PEOPLE in Time and Place

LIVING IN COMMUNITIES

SERIES CONSULTANTS

Dr. James F. Baumann
Professor of Reading Education
Associate Director, National Reading Research Center
The University of Georgia
Athens, GA

Dr. Theodore Kaltsounis
Professor of Social Studies Education
University of Washington
Seattle, WA

LITERATURE CONSULTANTS

Dr. Ben A. Smith
Assistant Professor of Social Studies Education
Kansas State University
Manhattan, KS

Dr. John C. Davis
Professor of Elementary Education
University of Southern Mississippi
Hattiesburg, MS

Dr. Jesse Palmer
Assistant Professor, Department of Curriculum and Instruction
University of Southern Mississippi
Hattiesburg, MS

SILVER BURDETT GINN

MORRISTOWN, NJ • NEEDHAM, MA
Atlanta, GA • Dallas, TX • Deerfield, IL • Menlo Park, CA

SERIES AUTHORS

Dr. W. Frank Ainsley, Professor of Geography, University of North Carolina, Wilmington, N C

Dr. Herbert J. Bass, Professor of History, Temple University, Philadelphia, PA

Dr. Kenneth S. Cooper, Professor of History, Emeritus, George Peabody College for Teachers, Vanderbilt University, Nashville, TN

Dr. Gary S. Elbow, Professor of Geography, Texas Tech University, Lubbock, TX

Roy Erickson, Program Specialist, K–12 Social Studies and Multicultural Education San Juan Unified School District, Carmichael, CA

Dr. Daniel B. Fleming, Professor of Social Studies Education, Virginia Polytechnic Institute and State University, Blacksburg, VA

Dr. Gerald Michael Greenfield, Professor and Director, Center for International Studies, University of Wisconsin — Parkside, Kenosha, WI

Dr. Linda Greenow, Associate Professor of Geography, SUNY – The College at New Paltz, New Paltz, NY

Dr. William W. Joyce, Professor of Education, Michigan State University, East Lansing, MI

Dr. Gail S. Ludwig, Geographer-in-Residence, National Geographic Society, Geography Education Program, Washington, D.C.

Dr. Michael B. Petrovich, Professor Emeritus of History, University of Wisconsin, Madison, WI

Dr. Arthur D. Roberts, Professor of Education, University of Connecticut, Storrs, CT

Dr. Christine L. Roberts, Professor of Education, University of Connecticut, Storrs, CT

Parke Rouse, Jr., Virginia Historian and Retired Executive Director of the Jamestown-Yorktown Foundation, Williamsburg, VA

Dr. Paul C. Slayton, Jr., Distinguished Professor of Education, Mary Washington College, Fredericksburg, VA

Dr. Edgar A. Toppin, Professor of History and Dean of the Graduate School, Virginia State University, Petersburg, VA

GRADE-LEVEL WRITERS/CONSULTANTS

Susan Barnes, Special Education Teacher, Pleasantville Elementary School, New Castle, DE

Joyce Kemp, Teacher Rio Grande School, Terre Haute, IN

Marva Waddell, Teacher, Kentopp Elementary School, East Orange, NJ

H. Hortense Ward, Teacher, Garfield Elementary School, Toledo, OH

Rhonda K. Allen, Former Teacher, Newark Public Schools, Newark, NJ

ACKNOWLEDGEMENTS

Excerpt from *Through Grandpa's Eyes* by Patricia MacLachlan © 1980 by Harper & Row, Inc. New York City. Used by permission of the publisher.

"Signs" by Ilo Orleans appeared in *Poems and Verses About the City,* 1968.

Featherboy and the Buffalo by Neil and Ting Morris. © 1984. Reprinted by permission of the publisher, Hodder & Stoughton Ltd. Kent, England.

3 4 5 6 7 8 9 – RRD – 99 98 97 96 95 94 93

ISBN 0-382-20936-2

CONTENTS

RESOURCE SECTION

MAPS

ATLAS

GRAPHS AND TIME LINES

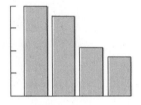

CHARTS AND DIAGRAMS

Special Features

Pen Pals

Literature

Citizenship and American Values

Skillbuilders

WE LEARN IN MANY WAYS

New Words

share

senses

group

What Do You Learn from Your Family?

When you were a baby, most things were done for you. As you grew, you learned many things. The first people you learned from were your family. Parents and other family members were your first teachers.

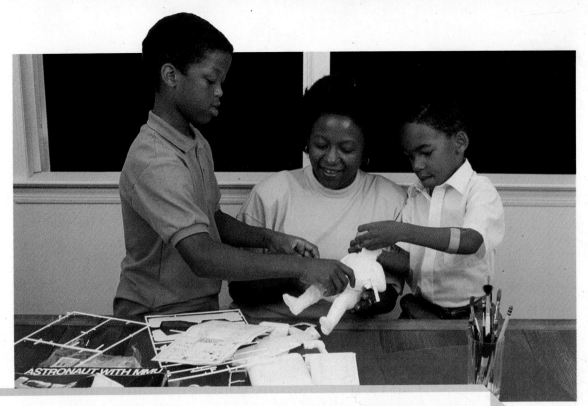

Family members learn from each other. They do things together. They **share** things. To share means to give what is yours to someone else.

Kate and her father are playing with the baby. "She is almost one year old," said Father. "It is time to teach her."

"I want to help teach her," said Kate.

"All right," Father said. "We will teach her a little each day. You get on one side, and I will get on the other."

Kate did as she was told. Together they helped the baby to stand up. They were all excited.

"Now," Father said, "let us try to get her to take a step."

Do you know what Kate and her father are doing? They are teaching the baby to walk. What are some other things the baby has to learn to do?

Review

Read and Think

1. Who are our first teachers?
2. What are some things family members teach us?
3. Who has helped you to learn?

Skills Check

Look at the pictures on pages 6 and 7.
What family members are teaching the baby?

What Do We Learn from Our Senses?

People are always learning. Every day there is something new to learn. Our **senses** help us learn about things. We use our senses to see, feel, smell, taste, and hear.

When we look at things, we are learning. Our eyes can see words and pictures. They can see shapes and colors. We learn many new things with our eyes.

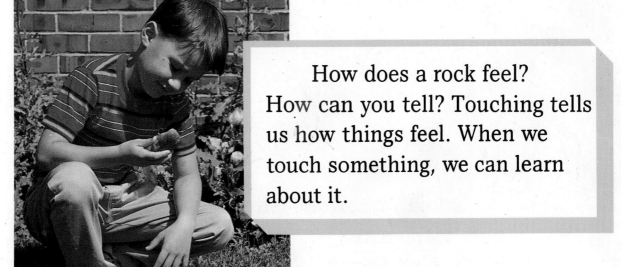

How does a rock feel? How can you tell? Touching tells us how things feel. When we touch something, we can learn about it.

We can learn about things by smelling. Our nose tells us how things smell. Some things smell good. Do you like the smell of baked bread?

Tasting is another way to learn. It tells us what we like to eat. All foods do not taste the same to all people.

We hear with our ears. When we listen, we hear sounds. The sounds tell us many things. Listening is one way of learning.

Review

Read and Think

1. For what do we use our senses?
2. What do we learn by tasting food?

Skills Check

Look at the pictures on pages 8 and 9.
Tell what is going on in each picture.

Through Grandpa's Eyes

by Patricia MacLachlan
pictures by Deborah Kogan Ray

This story is about John and his grandfather. John's grandfather is blind. In this story John tells how they wake up in the morning.

Of all the houses that I know, I like my grandpa's best. My friend Peter has a new glass house with pebble-path gardens that go nowhere. And Maggie lives next door in an old wooden house with rooms behind rooms, all with carved doors and brass doorknobs. They are fine houses. But Grandpa's house is my favorite. Because I see it through Grandpa's eyes.

Grandpa is blind. He doesn't see the house the way I do. He has his own way of seeing.

In the morning, the sun pushes through the curtains into my eyes. I burrow down into the covers to get away, but the light follows me. I give up, throw back the covers, and run to Grandpa's room.

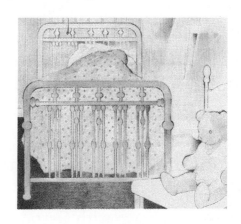

The sun wakes Grandpa differently from the way it wakes me. He says it touches him, *warming* him awake. When I peek around the door, Grandpa is already up and doing his morning exercises. Bending and stretching by the bed. He stops and smiles because he hears me.

"Good morning, John."

"Where's Nana?" I ask him.

"Don't you know?" he says, bending and stretching. "Close your eyes, John, and look through my eyes."

I close my eyes. Down below, I hear the banging of pots and the sound of water running that I didn't hear before.

"Nana is in the kitchen, making breakfast," I say.

When I open my eyes again, I can see Grandpa nodding at me. He is tall with dark gray hair. And his eyes are sharp blue even though they are not sharp seeing.

I exercise with Grandpa. Up and down. Then I try to exercise with my eyes closed.

"One, two," says Grandpa, "three, four."

"Wait!" I cry. I am still on one, two when grandpa is on three, four.

I fall sideways. Three times. Grandpa laughs as he hears my thumps on the carpet.

"Breakfast!" calls Nana from downstairs.

"I smell eggs frying," says Grandpa. He bends his head close to mine. "And buttered toast."

The wooden banister on the stairway has been worn smooth from Grandpa running his fingers up and down. I walk behind him, my fingers following Grandpa's smooth path.

We go into the kitchen.

"I smell flowers," says Grandpa.

"What flowers?" I ask.

He smiles. He loves guessing games.

"Not violets, John, not peonies . . ."

"Carnations!" I cry. *I* love guessing games.

"Silly." Grandpa laughs. "Marigolds. Right, Nana?"

Nana laughs, too.

"That's too easy," she says, putting two plates of food in front of us.

"It's not too easy," I protest. "How can Grandpa tell? All the smells mix together in the air."

"Close your eyes, John," says Nana. "Tell me what breakfast is."

"I smell the eggs. I smell the toast," I say, my eyes closed. "And something else. The something else doesn't smell good."

"*That* something else," says Nana, smiling, "is the marigolds."

When he eats, Grandpa's plate of food is a clock.

"Two eggs at nine o'clock and toast at two o'clock," says Nana to Grandpa. "And a dollop of jam."

"A dollop of jam," I tell Grandpa, "at six o'clock."

I make my plate of food a clock, too, and eat through Grandpa's eyes.

What Do You Think?

Think about the story you just read. Were you able to see through Grandpa's eyes, as John did? Do you think John and his grandfather have fun together?

Who Helps Us Learn in School?

We have learned many things at home. Now we are learning new things at school. Our teacher helps us learn. We learn to read and to count. Our spelling gets better. Our writing gets better. We work very hard in school. We also play and have fun.

We have books to help us learn
in school. Sometimes the teacher
reads to us. Sometimes we read alone.
Reading helps us to learn.

We learn a lot from school friends. They can talk. We can listen. We learn to take turns. We share things and learn to work and play together.

We sing and dance in school. The whole class takes part. We make all kinds of sounds. Our teacher helps us.

Review

Read and Think
1. Who helps us learn in school?
2. What do you like best about your school?

Skills Check
Look at the picture on page 20.
What do you think is going on in the picture?

What Can We Learn from Groups?

People like to be with other people. They like to do things together. When people do things together, they are part of a **group**.

People belong to many groups. A family is a group. It stays together for a long time. Sometimes people join groups to do special things. What kinds of groups are these?

Most boys and girls belong to a family group and a classroom group. Sometimes they join other special groups. Look at the chart. It shows some special groups children belong to.

Special Groups

	Reading	Cub Scouts	Ball Team	Brownies	Singing
Clara	✓			✓	✓
Sam	✓	✓	✓		
Erica	✓			✓	✓
Jay	✓	✓	✓		
Fran	✓		✓		

Look at this picture. What kind of group do these boys belong to?

Lesson 4 — Review

Read and Think

1. Why do people belong to groups?
2. What is a very special group?
3. What are three groups that you belong to?

Skills Check

Think of a group that you belong to. Write a short paragraph telling why you like the group.

A. Using the New Words

Find the picture that best matches each word.

1. share _____

2. senses _____

3. group _____

A.

B.

C.

B. Remembering What You Read

Answer these questions on a separate sheet of paper.

1. How do family members learn from each other?
2. What are some things you learn in school?
3. What are some groups you join to have fun?

C. Summarizing the Unit

Use the pictures to answer the questions.

1. What is each of these children learning?
2. Who is teaching each child?
3. Where is each child learning?

Using the Picture Glossary

A Why Do I Need This Skill?

In the back of your book is a Picture Glossary. It tells the meaning of each new word in this book. By using the Picture Glossary, you can find meanings of words quickly.

B Learning the Skill

Words in the Picture Glossary are in **ABC** order. The letters of the alphabet are in **ABC** order too. Words beginning with <u>a</u> come first. Next come words that start with <u>b</u>, then <u>c</u>, and so on. Each word has four parts. The parts are the word, its meaning, a picture, and a page number.

ABCDEFGHIJKLMNOPQRSTUVWXYZ
a b c d e f g h i j k l m n o p q r s t u v w x y z

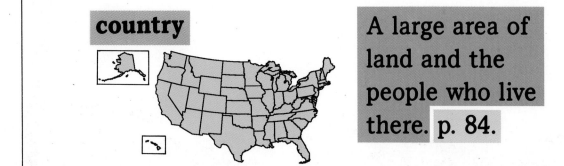

country

A large area of land and the people who live there. p. 84.

C Practicing the Skill

Turn to the Picture Glossary on page 222. Answer the following questions.

1. What is the first word shown?
2. On what page is the word first used in this book?

D Applying the Skill

Find the new words in Unit 1, on page 2. Find the same words in the Picture Glossary. Write down each word and its meaning. Use a separate sheet of paper.

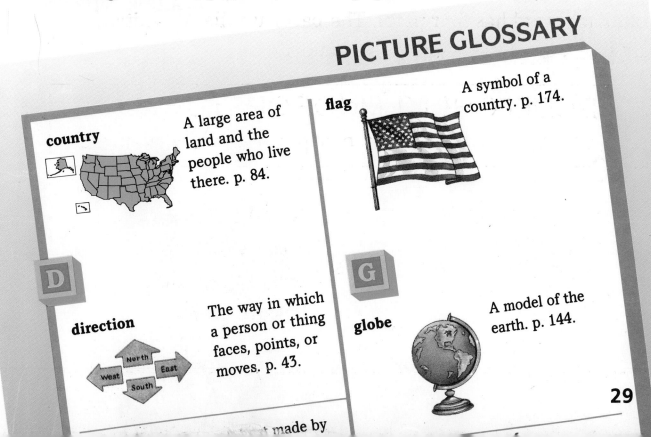

PICTURE GLOSSARY

country A large area of land and the people who live there. p. 84.

flag A symbol of a country. p. 174.

D

direction The way in which a person or thing faces, points, or moves. p. 43.

North
West East
South

G

globe A model of the earth. p. 144.

t made by

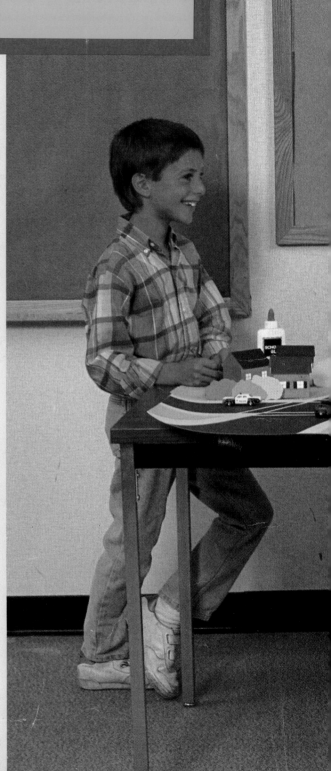

Unit 2 LEARNING ABOUT COMMUNITIES

New Words

community

neighborhood

map

Map Key

map key

symbol

city

transportation

suburb

direction

30

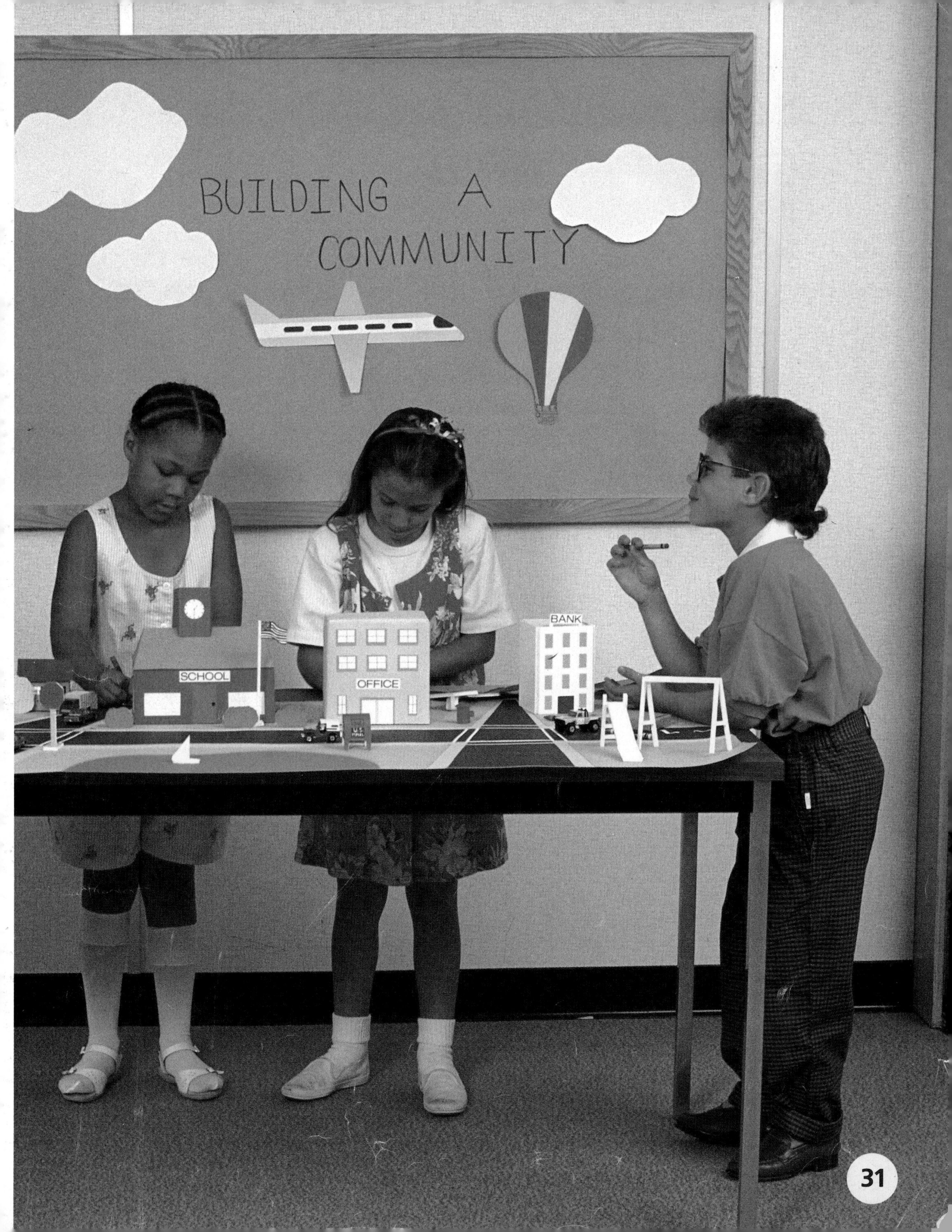
BUILDING A COMMUNITY
SCHOOL
OFFICE
BANK

What Is a Community?

This is a picture of a **community**. A community is a place where people live, work, and play. Some communities have many families. Other communities may have few families.

Communities are made up of different **neighborhoods**. A neighborhood is a place where people live near one another. The people who live in neighborhoods are neighbors. This picture shows some neighborhoods in a community.

A community has houses and other buildings. Some houses are for one family. Some are for two or more families.

Communities have special buildings and places. There may be libraries, schools, and different kinds of museums. In this museum, people can see works of art.

Review

Read and Think

1. What is a community?
2. Why do communities have special places?

Skills Check

Pick one photograph in this lesson. Write three sentences describing the photograph.

What Is a Map?

A community has places families like to visit. Lee and his parents are going to the zoo. On the next page is a **map** of the zoo. A map is a drawing of a place. The map will help the family to find things at the zoo.

A **map key** helps you read a map. The key tells you what map **symbols** mean. A symbol is a small picture or drawing that stands for a real thing. Look at the drawings in the map key. Can you tell what each symbol stands for?

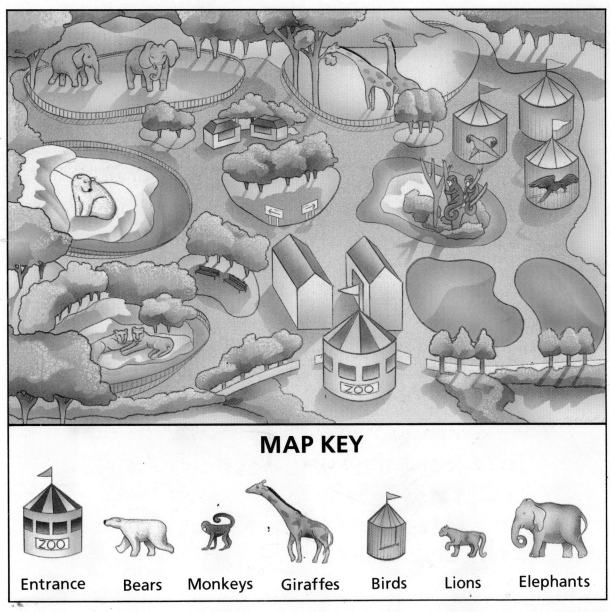

MAP KEY

| Entrance | Bears | Monkeys | Giraffes | Birds | Lions | Elephants |

Some symbols look like the things they stand for. Some do not.

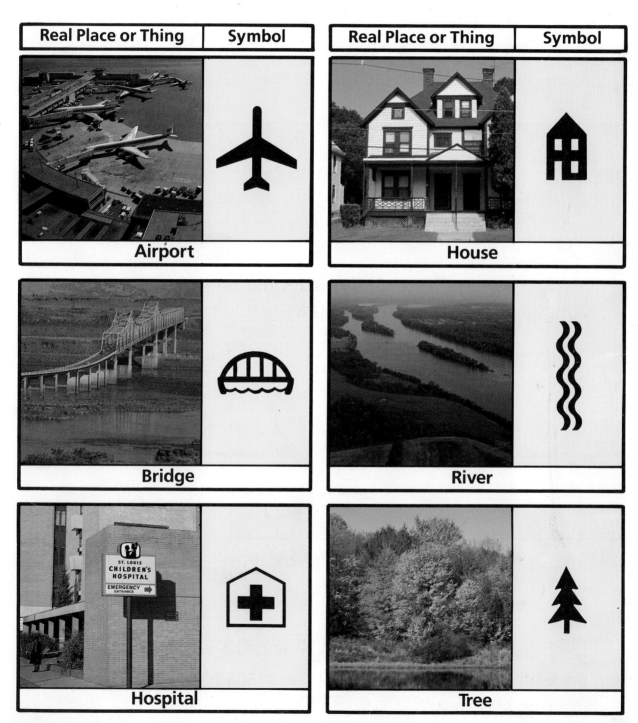

Real Place or Thing	Symbol	Real Place or Thing	Symbol
Airport		House	
Bridge		River	
Hospital		Tree	

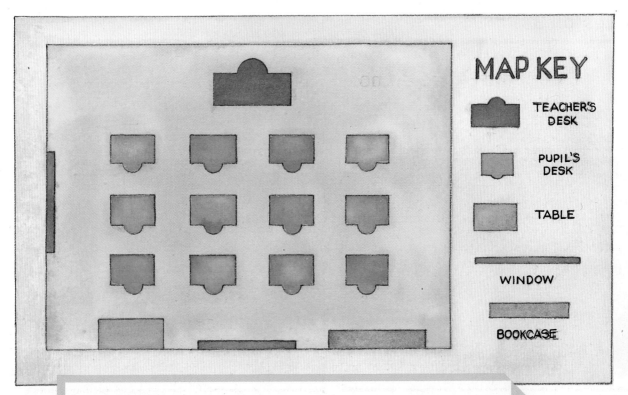

MAP KEY

- TEACHER'S DESK
- PUPIL'S DESK
- TABLE
- WINDOW
- BOOKCASE

This is a map of a classroom. How is it different from the map of the zoo?

Lesson 2

Review

Read and Think

1. What is a map?
2. What do symbols on a map stand for?

Skills Check

Look at the zoo map on page 37 and the classroom map on page 39. How are the two maps alike? How are they different?

How Is a Map Like a Photograph?

This photograph was taken from an airplane. It shows part of a community. Now look at the map on the next page. It shows the same areas as the photograph.

Use the map key. Find the color for the ball field.
Find the ball field on the map. Find it in the picture.

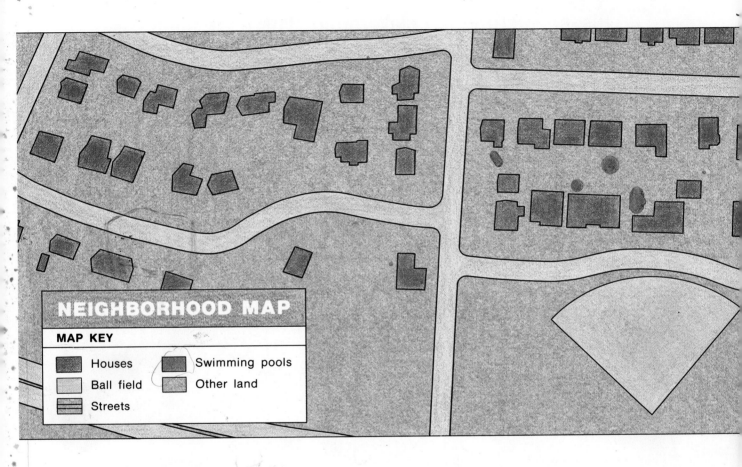

NEIGHBORHOOD MAP

MAP KEY

■	Houses	■	Swimming pools
■	Ball field	■	Other land
≡	Streets		

Lesson 3

Review

Read and Think

1. What do the photograph and map show?
2. Why does a map have a key?

Skills Check

Look at the photograph and the map. How are
they different? How are they the same?

41

What Are Direction Words?

This is a picture of a playground. There are many things to see. Find the slide. A boy is going <u>up</u> the ladder. A girl is going <u>down</u> the slide. Two children are sitting <u>under</u> a tree. Look at the <u>top</u> of the picture. Birds are flying <u>over</u> the playground. Look at the <u>bottom</u> of the picture. The girl has a balloon in her <u>left</u> hand. The boy has a ball in his <u>right</u> hand.

Some of the words on these pages have a line under them. These are all **direction** words. A direction word tells where something is. <u>Up</u>, <u>down</u>, <u>over</u>, and <u>under</u> are direction words. <u>Top</u>, <u>bottom</u>, <u>left</u>, and <u>right</u> are also direction words.

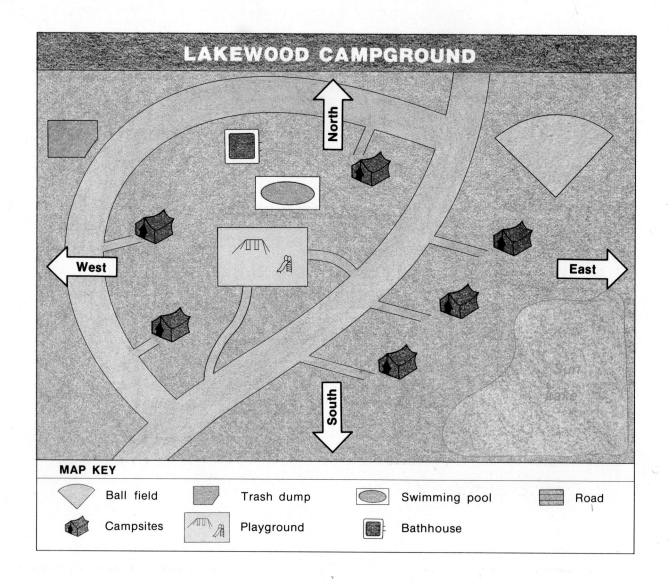

LAKEWOOD CAMPGROUND

MAP KEY

Ball field		Trash dump		Swimming pool		Road	
Campsites		Playground		Bathhouse			

Maps have four main directions. They are <u>north</u>, <u>south</u>, <u>east</u>, and <u>west</u>. The direction opposite north is south. East is opposite west. Look at the map and find the four directions.

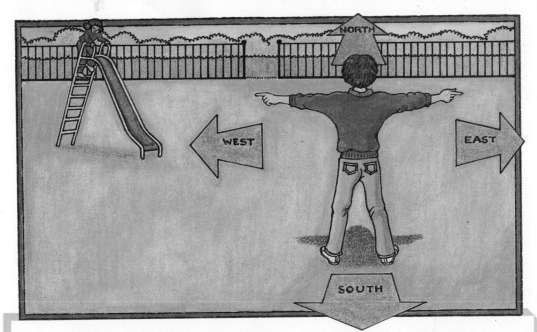

Your shadow can help you find directions. At noon, if you stand with your back to the sun, your shadow will point north. Your back will be toward the south. If you raise your arms, your left arm will point to the west. Your right arm will point to the east.

Lesson 4

Review

Read and Think

1. What are the four main directions?
2. If you know which way north is, how can you find west?

Skills Check

Look at the picture on pages 42 and 43. Write several sentences about the picture, using the words <u>up</u> and <u>down</u>.

Lesson 5
How Are Communities Alike and Different?

Communities are alike in many ways. They have houses, stores, and schools. They have streets and sidewalks. There are buildings for people to work in. There are places where people can have fun. What are some other ways communities are alike?

City

Communities are different in many ways too. Some communities are very large. A **city** is a large community.

Some communities are small. A town is a small community. Some towns have only one main street.

A **suburb** is a community near a city. Many people who live in a suburb work in a city. Some suburbs are big.

Town

Suburb

Communities can be found in many different places. They are found in hot, dry places. They are in cold, wet places. Some communities are near water. Some are on flat land, and some are on high land.

In some communities, neighbors live close together. In other communities they live far apart. Is your community like any of those shown in this lesson?

Review

Read and Think
1. What is one way communities are alike?
2. How are towns and suburbs different?

Skills Check
Look at the pictures on pages 48 and 49. How are these communities alike? How are they different?

What Is a City?

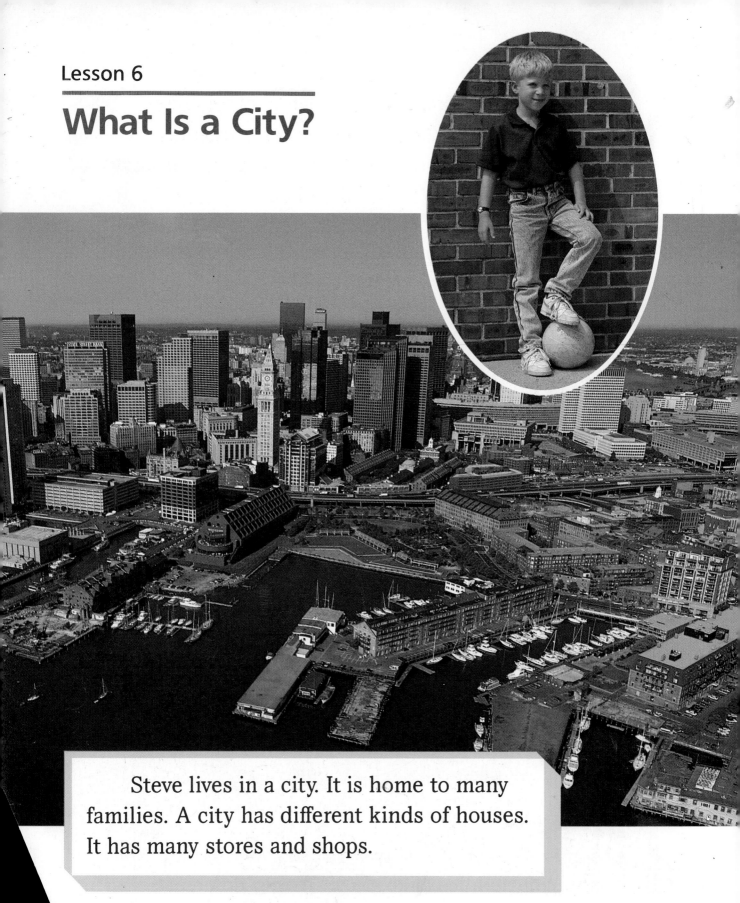

Steve lives in a city. It is home to many families. A city has different kinds of houses. It has many stores and shops.

Steve and his family live in a tall building. Many other families live in the same building. Each family has an apartment. An apartment may be one room or a group of rooms.

Steve can walk to school every day. But his parents need **transportation** to get to work. Transportation is the way people travel from one place to another. In big cities, many people use buses and subways to get around. A subway is a train that runs underground.

There are many fun things to do in a big city. Some cities have skating rinks like this one. Many people like to skate. Name some places to have fun in a city.

Review

Read and Think

1. What is Steve's community called?
2. What is Steve's building made of?

Skills Check

Look at the pictures on page 52. What other kinds of transportation are found in a city?

What Is a Farming Community?

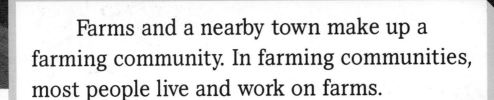

Farms and a nearby town make up a farming community. In farming communities, most people live and work on farms.

Cathy lives on a dairy farm. Her parents raise cows for milk. Their neighbors are dairy farmers too.

This is a drawing of the farm. Some of the places have been labeled. Find the barn in the drawing. Now find it in the picture on page 54.

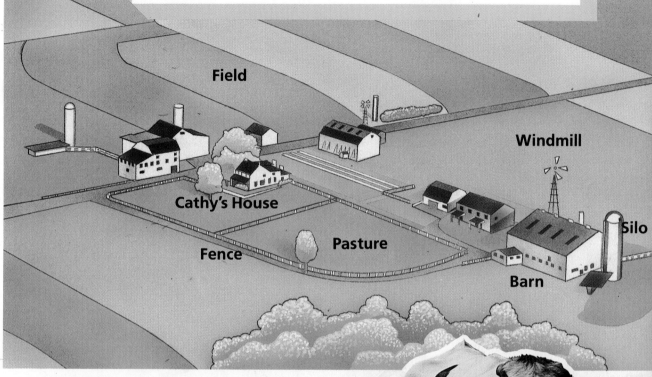

Field

Windmill

Silo

Cathy's House

Pasture

Fence

Barn

Dairy cows need a lot of grass and other foods. In the summer they graze in the pastures. In winter they eat hay and grain. The grain is kept in silos. Find the pastures and silos in the drawing. Find them in the picture.

People who live on farms often must go to town to shop. Sometimes they go to a shopping mall or nearby city.

Farming communities have many places to have fun. Cathy's family likes to have a picnic on the grass. Her brother likes to fish in the pond.

Review

Read and Think

1. What is a farm community near?
2. What are some animals found on a dairy farm?

Skills Check

Look at the picture on page 54. Why does a dairy farm need lots of land?

What Is a Suburb?

Jeff lives in a suburb. A suburb is a community near a large city. Find the city in this picture. Jeff's community has mostly houses. It has a few stores and shops.

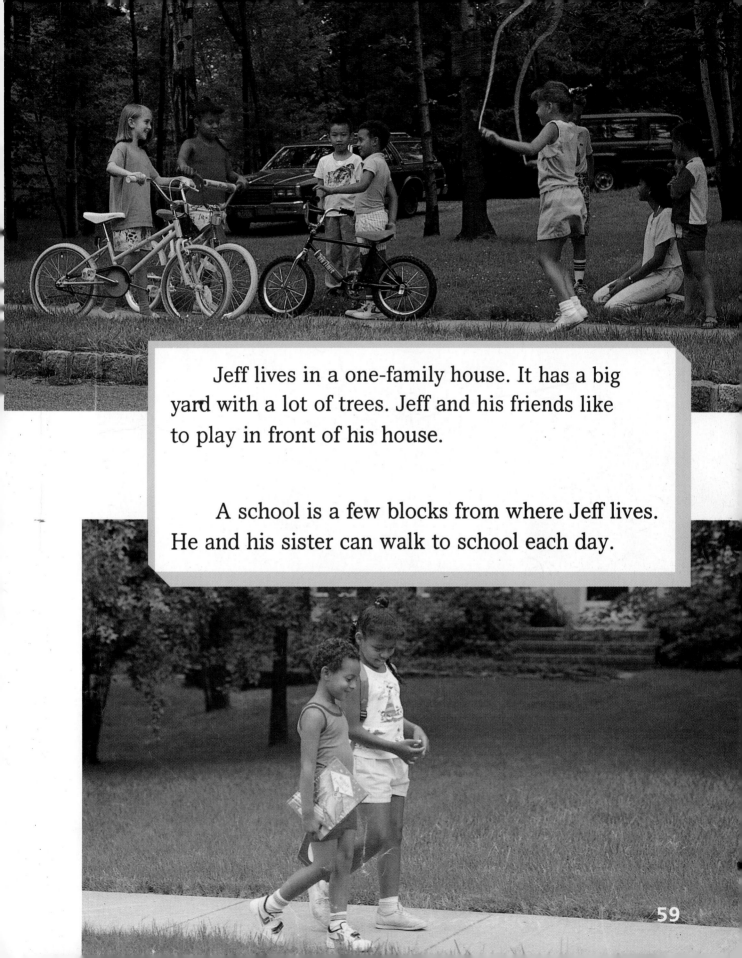

Jeff lives in a one-family house. It has a big yard with a lot of trees. Jeff and his friends like to play in front of his house.

A school is a few blocks from where Jeff lives. He and his sister can walk to school each day.

PEN PALS

Jeff has a pen pal. A pen pal is a friend you write to in another country. Jeff received a letter from his pen pal in Australia. Here is what Beth wrote to Jeff.

Dear Jeff,

My name is Beth. I live in Sydney, Australia. Sydney is a large city. It has many beautiful buildings. One of the best-known is the Opera House. It looks like a sea shell.

My home is near the water. My family and I can watch boat races from our window.

Write and tell me about where you live.

Your friend,
Beth

Jeff is writing a letter to Beth.
He wants to tell her about his community.

Lesson 8 ——— Review

Read and Think
1. What is a suburb?
2. What things do you enjoy in your community?

Skills Check
Look at the picture on page 58. What are some
things Jeff can tell Beth about his community?

A. Using the New Words

Find the picture that best matches each word.

1. community _____
2. neighborhood _____
3. map _____
4. symbol _____
5. map key _____
6. city _____
7. transportation _____
8. suburb _____
9. direction _____

A.

B.

C.

D.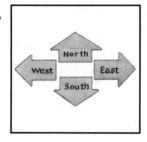

E.

F.

G.

Map Key
- House
- Lake
- Airport
- School

H.

I.

B. Remembering What You Read

1. What are buildings where many people live called?
2. How are cities and suburbs different?
3. Why do farming communities need a lot of land?

 # C. Summarizing the Unit

Look at the picture. Make a list of the different kinds of transportation you see.

SKILLBUILDER

Reading a Map

A Why Do I Need This Skill?

Maps are helpful tools. They are special drawings that show where things are. When you know how to use a map, you can find most places in the world.

B Learning the Skill

This is a map of a neighborhood. The map has different places. It uses symbols to show some of the places. Look at the map key. It tells what each symbol stands for.

The map also shows directions. Look at the four arrows on the map. They show north, south, east, and west. Directions can help you find where places are on the map.

West

C Practicing the Skill

Use the map and the map key to answer these questions.

1. What direction is opposite south?
2. What building is west of Cindy's house?
3. What does each symbol on the map stand for?
4. What direction is the school from the store?
5. What symbol stands for the park?

D Applying the Skill

Cindy walked from her house to the park. In which direction did she walk?

Key

school

Cindy's house

park

trees

fire station

police station

store

New Words

rule

law

leader

mayor

vote

state

governor

country

capitol building

Why Do Groups Have Rules?

Most groups have **rules**. Rules remind us what to do and what not to do. Rules help us work and play together. Some rules give us rights and responsibilities. Some help to keep us safe and healthy.

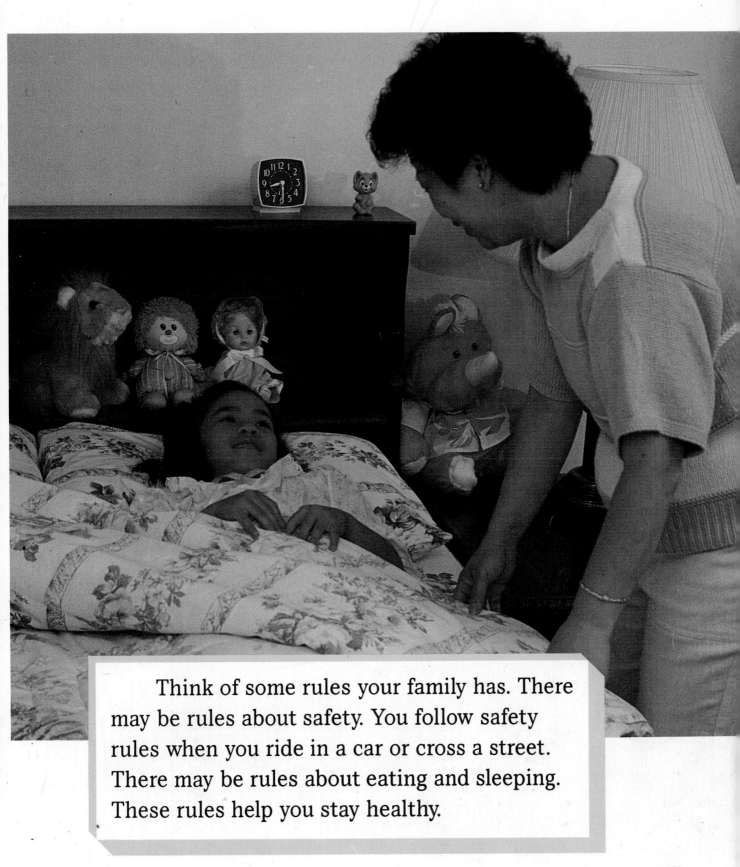

Think of some rules your family has. There may be rules about safety. You follow safety rules when you ride in a car or cross a street. There may be rules about eating and sleeping. These rules help you stay healthy.

Schools have rules too. We follow rules when we play together. We follow rules in our classroom. School rules make it easier for everyone to learn. They help us get along together.

Workers follow rules on their jobs. There are rules that protect them from being hurt. There are rules about doing their jobs. There are rules to help them get along with one another.

Review

Read and Think

1. Name two groups that have rules.
2. What is a rule your family has?

Skills Check

Look at the pictures on this page. What might happen if the rules were not followed?

What Are Community Laws?

Communities have rules. Community rules are called **laws**. Everyone must obey community laws. They help to protect the rights of people. Some community laws are about health and safety. Some help to protect property.

We cannot always remember all the rules and laws we must follow. Signs help us to remember. Signs remind us of what we should or should not do.

This poem is about some signs we might see when we are riding in a car.

SIGNS

When I went riding
  Yesterday,
I watched the signs
  Along the way.

"No Parking"; "Exit";
  "To the Zoo";
"Traffic Circle";
  "Fifth Avenue";

"Stay in Line";
  And "Stop" and "Go";
"Tunnel"; "Bridge";
  "Steep Hill"; "Go Slow";

"No Trucks"; "One Way";
  "No Turns"; "Keep Right";
The signs are everywhere
  In sight!

I read out loud
  Each sign I saw,
So daddy should
  Obey the law!

—Ilo Orleans

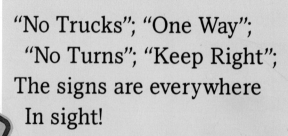

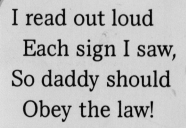

How will these children know
when it is safe to cross the street?

Lesson 2 ━━━━━━━ **Review** ━━━━━━━

Read and Think
1. Why do we have rules?
2. What are some signs in your neighborhood?

Skills Check
Write a short paragraph telling why it is important
to obey signs.

Who Makes Community Rules and Laws?

Do you know who makes laws in a community? Some communities have a group of community **leaders** who make their laws. Leaders are people who help to run the community.

In most communities the **mayor** is the chief leader. Other leaders help the mayor watch over the community.

Many community leaders are chosen by the people of a community. The people **vote** for their leaders. You can see a voting machine in this picture. The people who get the most votes become leaders.

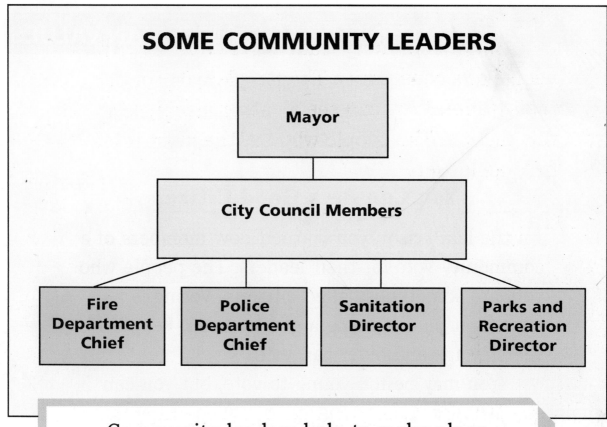

SOME COMMUNITY LEADERS

Mayor

City Council Members

Fire Department Chief • Police Department Chief • Sanitation Director • Parks and Recreation Director

Community leaders help to make plans and laws for the community. They work to solve problems in the community. They try to make the community a pleasant place to live.

Lesson 3

Review

Read and Think

1. Who makes laws in a community?
2. Who chooses community leaders?

Skills Check

Look at the picture on page 78. What is the person in the picture doing?

You Can Be a Good Citizen

In the last lesson you learned how members of a community vote for their leaders. The people who vote are sometimes called citizens. Voting is an important part of being a good citizen. People 18 years of age and older can vote.

You may be too young to vote, but you can still be a good citizen. A good citizen obeys rules and laws. There are rules at home. There are rules at school. Some rules are made to help you get along with others. Some are made to keep you healthy and safe from harm. When you obey rules, you are being a good citizen.

A good citizen obeys community laws too. You have seen traffic signs that say Stop or Do Not Walk. You have also seen signs like the one below. They remind us of community laws. When you obey these laws, you are being a good citizen.

Thinking for Yourself

Good citizens try to make their community a better place to live. List some ways you can make your community a better place.

What Is a State?

Your community is a part of a **state**. A state is made up of many communities. In what state is your community?

This map shows the state of Oregon. There are many communities in Oregon. Some are large, and some are small. Oregon has a special city. It is called the state capital. Find Oregon's state capital on the map.

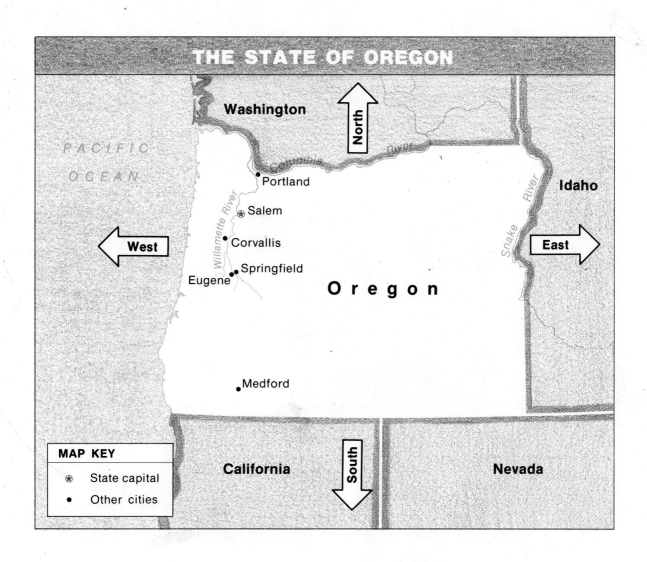

THE STATE OF OREGON

Washington

PACIFIC OCEAN

North

Columbia River

Portland

Willamette River

Salem

Corvallis

West

Springfield

Eugene

Oregon

Snake River

Idaho

East

Medford

MAP KEY

⊛ State capital

• Other cities

California

South

Nevada

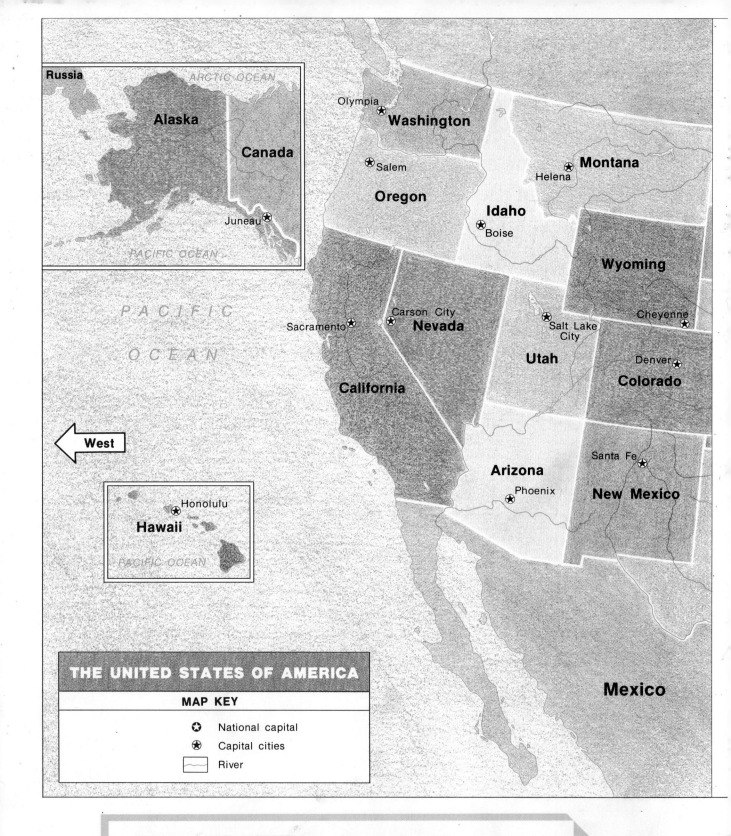

Our **country** has 50 states. Your state is one of the 50 states.

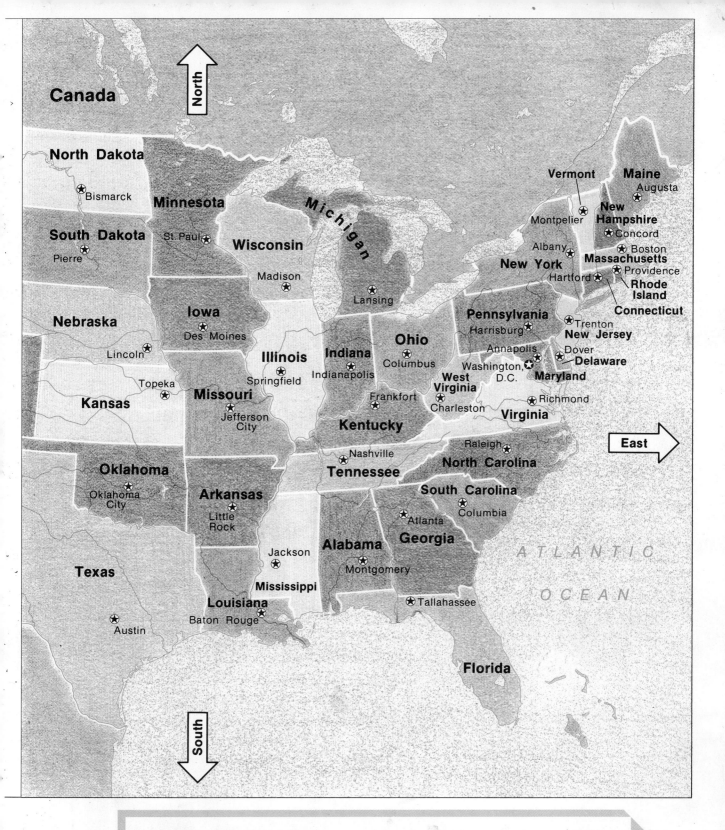

Each state has a capital city. Laws and plans for the state are made in the capital city.

Each state has its own leaders. The leaders make laws to help and to protect all the people in the state. The **governor** is the most important leader. The governor is elected by the people of the state.

The governor and other state leaders work in the **capitol building.** This capitol building is in the state of New Jersey.

Lesson 4 ——— Review ———

Read and Think

1. How many parts does our country have?
2. Why do states need leaders?

Skills Check

Look at the map on pages 84–85. Name the capital cities of Florida, Utah, Iowa, and West Virginia.

A. Using the New Words

Find the picture that best matches each word.

1. rule _____ I
2. law _____ C
3. leader _____ A
4. mayor _____ H
5. vote _____ G
6. state _____ D
7. country _____ E
8. governor _____ F
9. capitol building _____ B

A.

B.

C.

D.

E.

F.

G.

H.

I.

88

B. Remembering What You Read

1. What are two things that rules do?
2. Who is the leader of a state?
3. What are two rules at your school?

C. Summarizing the Unit

Some signs have no words. Look at these signs. What do the signs tell us? Where do you see signs like these?

SKILLBUILDER
Following Written Directions

A Why Do I Need This Skill?

Written directions are steps for doing something. People use written directions to put things together. You follow written directions to do your homework. Following written directions often helps us do things the right way.

B Learning the Skill

Look at the list below. What do these directions tell you to do? Where would you find each of these directions?

1. Please write neatly.
2. Do not litter.
3. Walk quietly in the hallways.
4. Please be quiet.
5. Keep dogs on a leash.

Practicing the Skill

Follow these written directions. Read them carefully. Check your work when you are finished.

1. Print your name.

2. Write the name of your favorite color.

3. Write the name of your favorite food.

4. Write the name of your state.

5. Write the name of your favorite city.

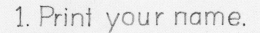

Applying the Skill

Look for written directions in your home or school. Remember what directions you see. Share what you find with your teacher and classmates.

WORKING IN COMMUNITIES

New Words

wants

product

service

taxes

basic needs

income

budget

graph

factory

92

What Are Needs and Wants?

All people must have certain things to live. They must have food, clothing, and homes. We call these things **basic needs**. A basic need is something people cannot do without. The three basic needs are the same for all people wherever they live.

People have other needs too. They need
friends. They need love and understanding.
They need to have fun.

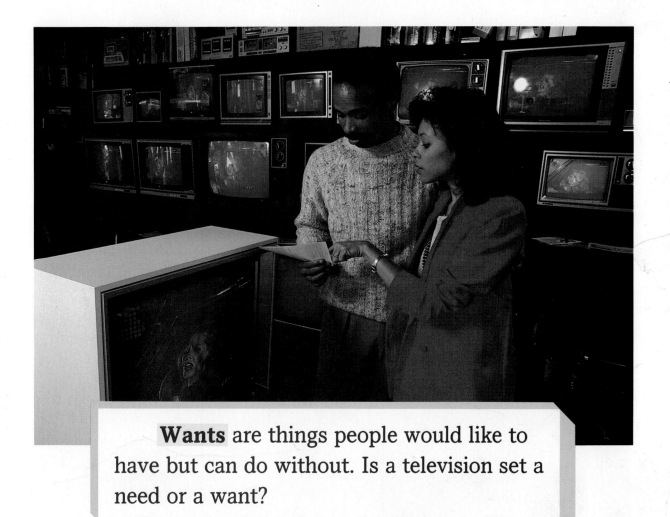

Wants are things people would like to have but can do without. Is a television set a need or a want?

Lesson 1

Review

Read and Think
1. What are the three basic needs?
2. What are wants?
3. What are some other things people need?

Skills Check

Look at the pictures on pages 94 and 95. Which things do you need to live?

How Do People Earn and Spend Their Money?

People earn money for the work they do. The money is called **income**. Income is used to buy the things people need and want.

There are many kinds of jobs. Some workers make the things we use. Some workers grow the foods we eat. Something that is made or grown is called a **product**. Name these products.

Some workers do things for other people. They provide, or give, **services**. A service is a kind of work that helps people. Name these workers. What services do they provide?

Families use some of their income to buy the things they need and want. They save money too. To save money means to put it away. Mrs. Lopez saves her money in a bank. A bank keeps money safe for people.

The Lopez family is setting up a **budget**. A budget is a spending plan. It will help the family save for things they need and want.

Look at the pie **graph**. It shows how the Lopez family budgets its money. The whole graph stands for the family's income for a month.

Pie Graph

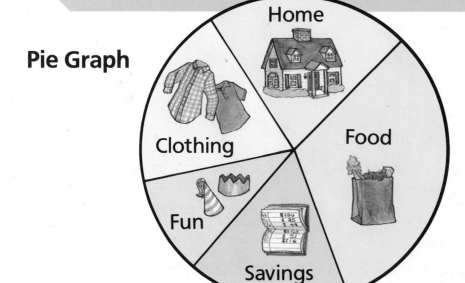

The Lopez family is saving money for a special reason. They want to take a trip. They will save until they have enough money.

Review

Read and Think

1. What is a budget?
2. What is something you might want to save money for?

Skills Check

Look at the pie graph on page 102. What is most of the family's income used for?

Who Are Community Workers?

Families want to live in a community where they can get the services they need. All the people in these pictures work for a community. They help to make life better for families in the community. Can you name these workers?

Families pay money to their community. The money is called **taxes**. The community pays its workers with money collected from taxes.

PAY TAXES HERE

This community worker makes sure our water is clean and safe to drink.

Lesson 3 — Review

Read and Think

1. What are taxes?
2. Name a community service worker and tell what that worker does.

Skills Check

Look at the pictures on pages 104 and 105. How do these workers help a community?

How Is a School Bus Made?

A school bus is a product. It is made in a **factory**. A factory is a place where most products are made. It takes many workers to make a school bus. This lesson shows you how workers make a school bus.

1. Each bus begins with a set of plans. This worker is looking at the plans on a computer.

2. Workers build the bus frame and wrap the frame in sheets of steel.

3. The bus is being spray-painted. Most school buses are painted yellow.

4. The seats are made of foam padding and wood.

5. The seats are bolted to the floor.

6. A stop sign is put on the left side of the bus.

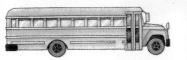

7. Mirrors are put on the left side and the right side. They help the driver to see behind the bus.

8. Lights are put on the front of the bus.

9. Windshield wipers are put on and tested.

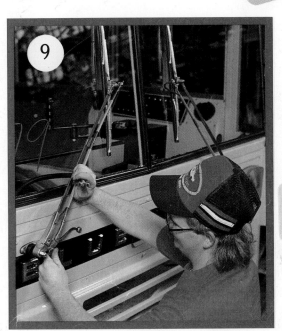

111

10. Workers are putting the motor in the bus.

11. The body of the bus is water tested for leaks.

12. These children have had a safe and comfortable ride on the new school bus.

<u>Lesson 4</u> ━━━━━━━ **Review** ━━━━━━━

Read and Think

1. What is a factory?
2. How do mirrors help bus drivers?
3. What do factory workers earn for the work they do?

Skills Check

Look at the pictures on page 109. Why, do you think, do these workers wear special clothing?

A. Using the New Words

Find the picture that best matches each word.

1. product _____

2. service _____

3. income _____

4. taxes _____

5. factory _____

6. budget _____

7. graph _____

8. basic needs _____

9. wants _____

A.

B.

C.

D.

E.

F.

G.

H.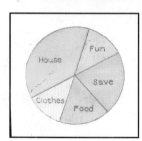

I.

114

B. Remembering What You Read

1. What needs do all people have?
2. How do communities pay their workers?
3. What is one thing you would like to save for?

C. Summarizing the Unit

Look at the picture. Which things do all people need to live? What are the other things in the picture called?

Why Do I Need This Skill?

Finding the main ideas will help you understand your social studies book better.

Learning the Skill

Every story has a main idea. Writers sometimes put the main idea in one sentence. The other, smaller ideas tell about the main idea. These are called details. Read the next paragraph. The main idea is underlined.

<u>People have three basic needs.</u> They need food to eat. They need clothing to wear. They need homes to live in.

Look at the umbrella on the next page. It acts like a main idea. It covers all the details that go with the main idea. Think of an umbrella when you look for main ideas.

Practicing the Skill

Find the main idea in the next paragraph. Draw an umbrella and write the main idea on it. Then add the details.

People have other needs too. They need friends. They need love. They need to have fun.

116

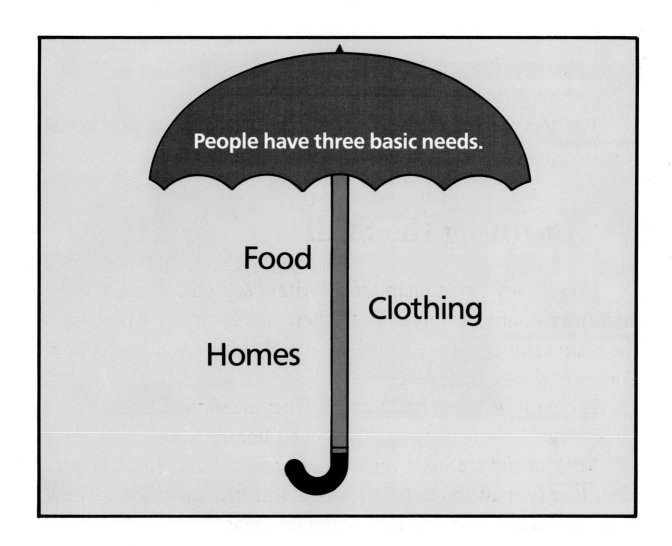

People have three basic needs.

Food

Clothing

Homes

 ## Applying the Skill

Look for main idea sentences when you read the next unit. It is about communities of long ago. Think of an umbrella to help you understand how main ideas and details work together.

COMMUNITIES OF LONG AGO

New Words

dugout canoe

natural resources

settlement

buffalo

pioneer

tribe

settler

Who Were the First Americans?

American Indians were the first people to live in this country. They lived in special groups called **tribes**. Most Indian tribes lived in villages. A village is a small community.

Not all Indian tribes were the same. They had different names and different ways of doing things. Indian tribes used the **natural resources** around them to meet their basic needs. Natural resources are things found in nature, such as land, trees, and water.

The Seneca tribes lived in the woods. They used the trees and tree bark to build their long houses. The Senecas planted corn and beans. They hunted and fished. They made their clothes from the skins of animals.

The Hopi tribes lived in the desert. They lived in what is today the state of Arizona. Their homes were built from rocks and mud. The Hopi Indians were farmers. They grew vegetables such as corn, beans, and squash. Clothing was made from the wool of sheep.

The Chinook tribes lived near the water. Large trees grew nearby. The Chinooks used the trees to build their homes. They built **dugout canoes** for fishing. The canoes were made from tree trunks. The Chinooks also hunted. They used animal skins and furs to make their clothing.

The Sioux lived on the plains. They were hunters. Their homes were called tepees. A tepee was made by putting **buffalo** skins around long poles. The Sioux used nearly every part of the buffalo. They ate buffalo meat. They used buffalo skins to make their clothing.

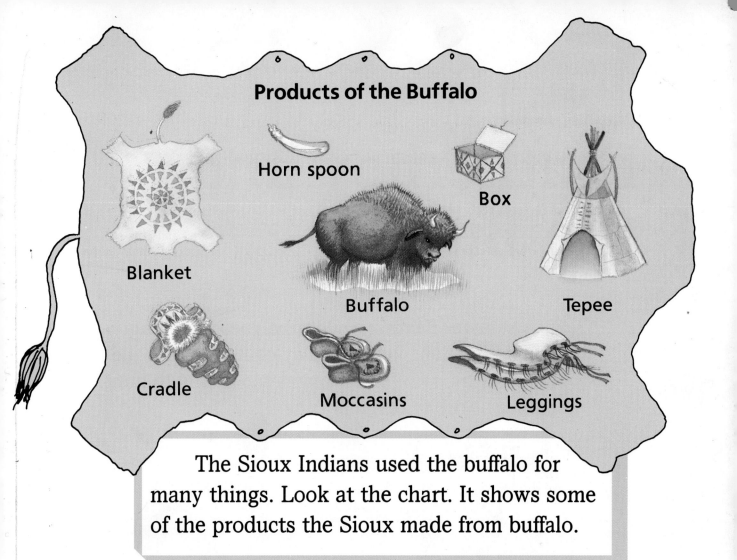

Products of the Buffalo

Horn spoon

Box

Blanket

Buffalo

Tepee

Cradle

Moccasins

Leggings

The Sioux Indians used the buffalo for many things. Look at the chart. It shows some of the products the Sioux made from buffalo.

Lesson 1 — Review

Read and Think

1. Who were the first people to live in this country?
2. In what ways did Seneca tribes live differently from Hopi tribes?

Skills Check

Look at the chart above. Copy the names of products made from the buffalo and put the words in alphabetical order.

Featherboy and the Buffalo

by Neil and Ting Morris
pictures by Anna Clarke

Each summer Featherboy's tribe goes on a long buffalo hunt. One summer they could not find the buffalo. Although Featherboy is too young to hunt, he finds a way to help his tribe.

Every spring groups of Sioux Indians traveled to their tribe's summer camp for the big buffalo hunt. Featherboy and Eagle-Eye were too young to hunt, but they looked forward to the exciting days ahead.

After their long ride the two boys were glad to see the smoke from the distant tepees. They thought of all the new friends they would make as they rode into camp.

But they were not given the usual warm welcome. There seemed to be a worried look on every face, and they wondered what could be wrong.

As Featherboy helped to put up their tepee, he heard another woman telling his mother about the problem. The hunters could not find any buffalo this year, and there was very little food left in the camp.

Next day the boys went off to join in a game with their friends. But Featherboy kept thinking about the gloom that hung over them.

Later he decided to explore beyond the camp. As it grew dark, he met the hunters returning. He could see from their faces that they had found no buffalo.

Early next morning Featherboy's father left with the hunters. Perhaps my father will bring them luck, he thought. Meanwhile he and Eagle-Eye went off with their friends to catch rabbits.

They stopped at a waterfall and splashed about in the icy water. Suddenly Featherboy saw three crows flying above him. It looked as if they were heading off into the hills.

Featherboy felt he had to follow the crows. They seemed to be leading him to the top of a hill, as if he would find something there.

Perhaps he would see buffalo in the valley below? Featherboy rushed on to the hilltop, but when he got there all he could see were rocks and bushes.

Featherboy was tired and disappointed. He lay down under a tree to rest and soon fell asleep. He was awakened by the crows. When he saw them pecking at the juicy berries, he realized how hungry he was. He could pick some berries too — perhaps even take some back to camp.

Behind the bushes was a gaping hole, and at once Featherboy saw a great herd of buffalo. When he found a black feather, he remembered the crows and thought they must have shown him the way. He picked up the feather and rushed back to the camp to tell everyone of his discovery. Featherboy was able to tell his father exactly where the buffalo were.

Featherboy's father took him at once to the chief's lodge. The chief and his hunters were preparing for a ceremony to help them find the buffalo. Now there would be a celebration instead!

That night the hunters danced in praise of the buffalo spirit. To thank him for his discovery, Featherboy was given a place of honor next to the chief.

Early next morning the hunters moved in for the kill. Although Featherboy, Eagle-Eye and the other boys were too young to hunt, they were very excited as they waited for their chance to help skin the buffalo.

The hunt was a great success, and now there was plenty of food for the whole tribe. As Featherboy sat and ate, he secretly thanked the crows for leading him and his people to the buffalo.

What Do You Think?

What might have happened to the tribe if Featherboy had not found the herd of buffalo? Would you like to go on a buffalo hunt? Tell why or why not.

How Did Settlements Begin?

Many years ago people from other places came to this land. They came from England, Spain, and other countries. These people were the first settlers. A **settler** was a person who came from another country to live in America.

The settlers were happy to be in America. They started **settlements**. A settlement is a small community. Soon there were settlements all along the eastern part of our country.

131

As the country grew, **pioneers** started moving west. A pioneer is a person who leads the way to a new land. The pioneers cleared the forest and started new settlements.

Soon there were fishing communities and farming communities all over our country. Some small settlements grew into big cities. The picture above shows Baltimore, Maryland, when it was a small settlement.

Lesson 2

Review

Read and Think

1. Who were the settlers?
2. How did the pioneers travel west?

Skills Check

Look at the picture on this page. How did the people in this settlement make a living?

What Were Schools like Long Ago?

Long ago there were no school buildings. Pioneer children went to the teacher's home to be taught. The children sat around the fireplace. Most families did not have money. They paid the teacher with food or clothes.

The children learned to read and to write. They had to share everything. There were never enough books and paper for everyone. Soon there were too many children for a teacher's house. Families in a settlement got together and built a small schoolhouse.

The first schoolhouses had one room. All grades were in the same room. Children shared desks and books. Older children helped to teach the younger ones.

Today, many people like to visit this school. It is the oldest wooden schoolhouse in our country. This schoolhouse is in St. Augustine, Florida. Find Florida on the map on page 85.

Lesson 3 — Review

Read and Think

1. Where did some children go to school long ago? **(Recall)**
2. How is your school different from schools of long ago? **(Analyze)**

Skills Check

Look at the picture on pages 134 and 135. Describe what you see in the picture.

A. Using the New Words

Find the picture that best matches each word.

1. tribe _____
2. natural resources _____
3. buffalo _____
4. dugout canoe _____
5. settlement _____
6. pioneer _____
7. settler _____

A.

B.

C.

D.

E.

F.

G.

B. Remembering What You Read

1. Who were the first Americans?
2. What were American Indian communities called?
3. What are some natural resources you use every day?

 C. Summarizing the Unit

Natural resources are things found in nature. What natural resources do you see in this picture?

SKILLBUILDER

Compare and Contrast

A Why Do I Need This Skill?

To compare is to see how things are alike. To contrast is to see how things are different. Comparing and contrasting are good ways to learn about the things around you.

B Learning the Skill

Look at these two pictures below. What do they show? What are some things that are in both pictures? When you answer these questions, you are comparing.

Look at the pictures again. What things are not the same in both? What does one picture have that the other does not? When you answer these questions, you are contrasting.

Practicing the Skill

Look at the pictures on pages 122 and 123. Find some ways the two villages are alike and different.

Applying the Skill

Compare and contrast these two pictures. Make a list of the ways the pictures are alike. List the ways they are different.

COMMUNITIES AROUND THE WORLD

New Words

ocean

globe

mountain

continent

hill

island

river

lake

142

Where Do We Live?

We live on the earth. The earth is home to all people. This picture shows a **globe**. A globe is a model of the earth. A globe shows where places are on the earth.

A globe can help you find directions. North is the direction toward the North Pole. Find the North Pole. South is the direction toward the South Pole. Find the South Pole. The North Pole and the South Pole are opposite each other.

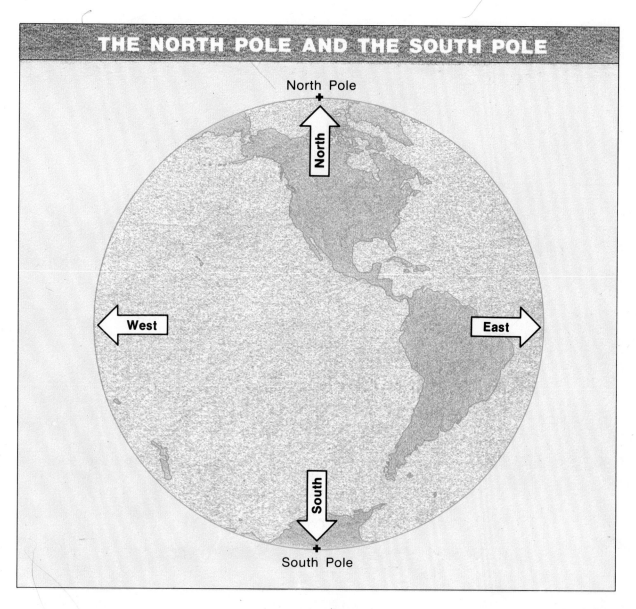

THE NORTH POLE AND THE SOUTH POLE

North Pole
North

West

East

South

South Pole

The earth is made of land and water. There are different kinds of bodies of water. A **lake** is a body of water with land all around it. A **river** is a long body of water that flows into a larger body of water. An **ocean** is a large body of salt water. The drawing shows some kinds of land and water.

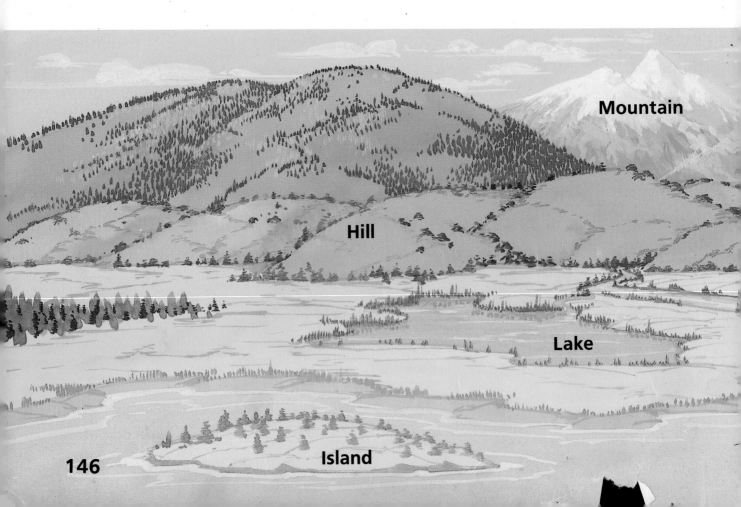

Mountain

Hill

Lake

Island

There are different kinds of land on the earth. One kind of land is an **island**. An island has water all around it. Another kind of land is a **hill**. A hill is higher than the land around it. A **mountain** is very high land. It also rises above the land around it. A mountain is higher than a hill.

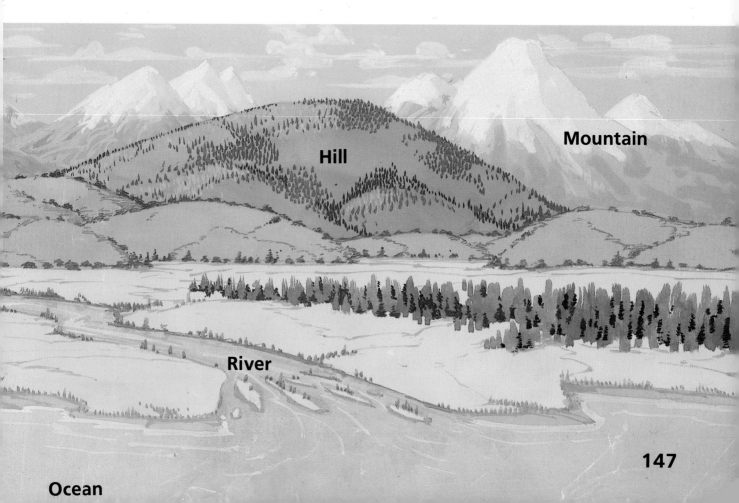

Mountain

Hill

River

Ocean

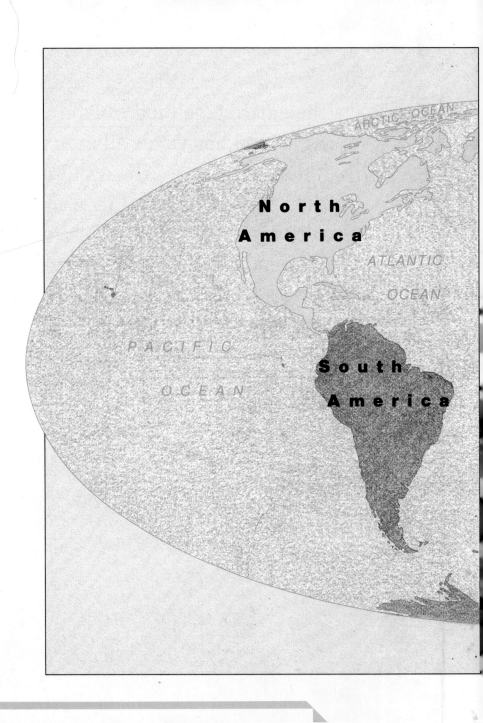

This is a map of the world. It shows oceans and **continents**. An ocean is a large body of salt water. There are four oceans. A continent is a large land area. There are seven continents.

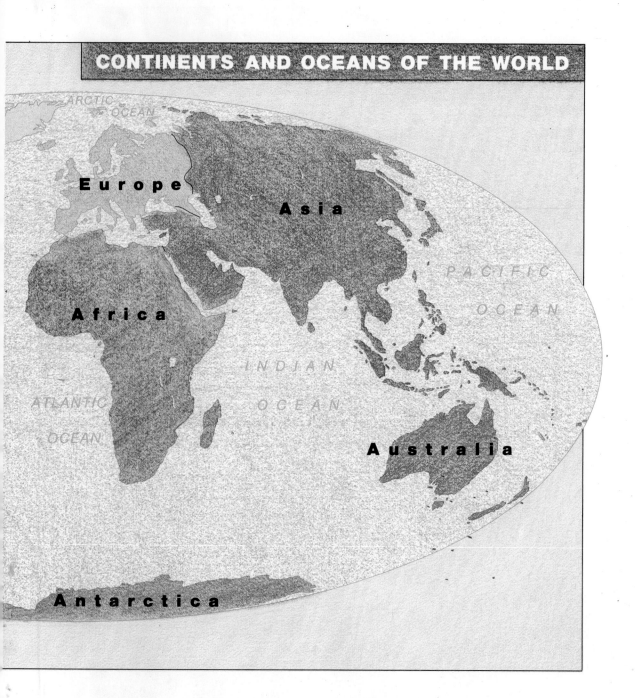

CONTINENTS AND OCEANS OF THE WORLD

ARCTIC OCEAN

Europe

Asia

PACIFIC OCEAN

Africa

INDIAN OCEAN

ATLANTIC OCEAN

Australia

Antarctica

THE CONTINENT OF NORTH AMERICA

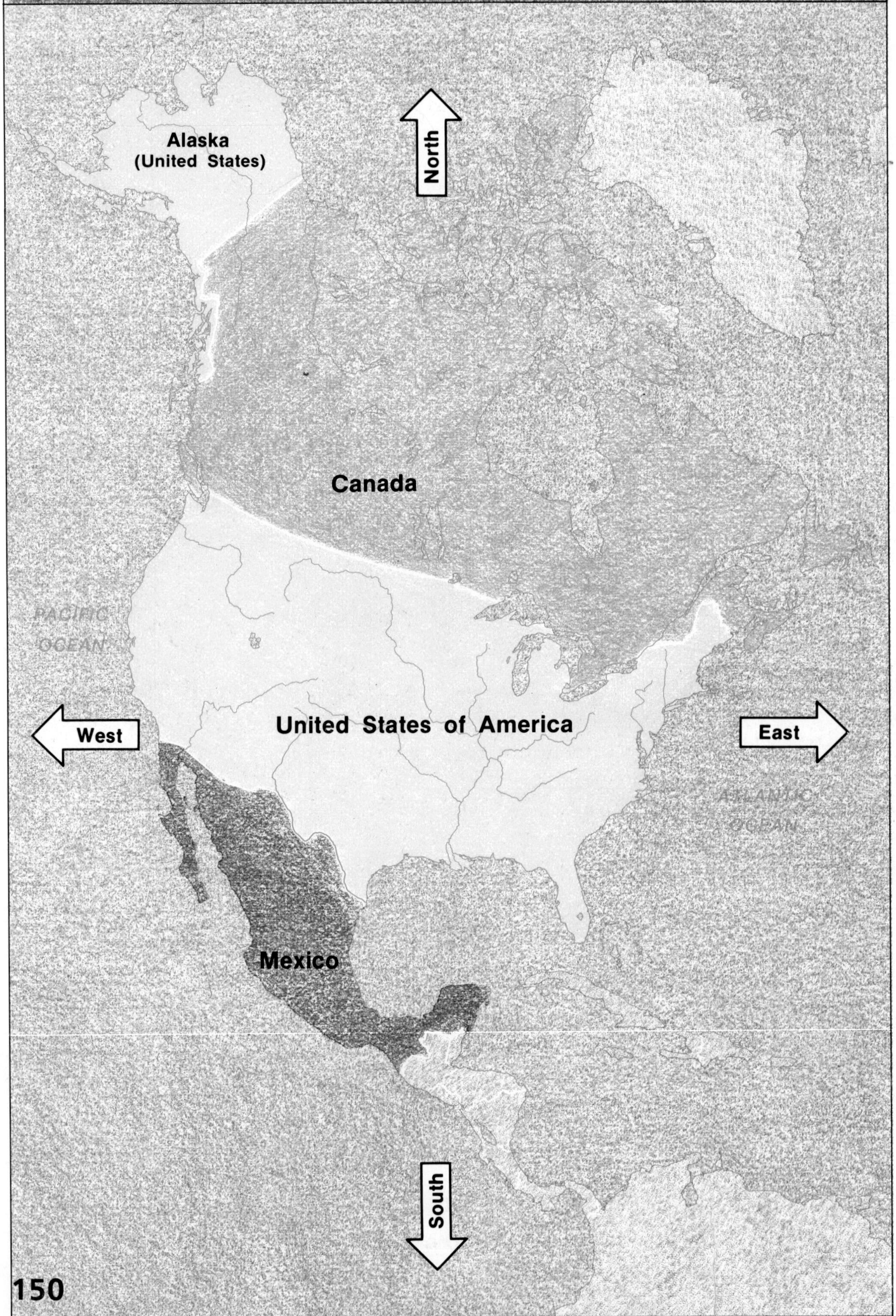

Alaska
(United States)

North

Canada

PACIFIC
OCEAN

West

United States of America

East

ATLANTIC
OCEAN

Mexico

South

Look at the map of North America. It is the continent we live on. Canada and Mexico are also in North America.

The picture below shows part of the Niagara Falls. Niagara Falls has waterfalls in the United States and in Canada.

Lesson 1

Review

Read and Think

1. What is a globe? (Recall)
2. How are the earth and the globe alike? (Evaluate)

Skills Check

Look at the map on pages 148 and 149. Which continent is closest to North America?

Where Is Masako's Community?

THE UNITED STATES AND JAPAN

Japan

Tokyo

United States

Masako lives in Japan. Japan is an island country. It is part of Asia. Tokyo is Japan's biggest city. It is also the capital of Japan.

Masako and her family live in a suburb of Tokyo. They have a house with a garden in the back. The garden has rocks, flowers, and small trees. In the middle of the garden is a pond. Nearly all the people in Masako's neighborhood have beautiful gardens.

Masako and her family go to Tokyo to shop. There are many different kinds of stores. People from all over the world like to visit Tokyo.

Sometimes Masako and her family visit a petting zoo. At a petting zoo children can touch some of the animals.

Lesson 2
Review

Read and Think

1. Which continent is Japan a part of?
2. What kinds of animals might be found in a petting zoo?

Skills Check

Look at the picture on this page. How is this zoo different from a zoo you have visited?

Where Is Kareem's Community?

THE UNITED STATES AND LIBERIA

This is the city of Monrovia, Liberia. Liberia is a country in Africa. Monrovia is on the ocean. It is the largest city in Liberia.

PEN PALS

Kareem lives in Monrovia. He likes to write to his pen pals in America.

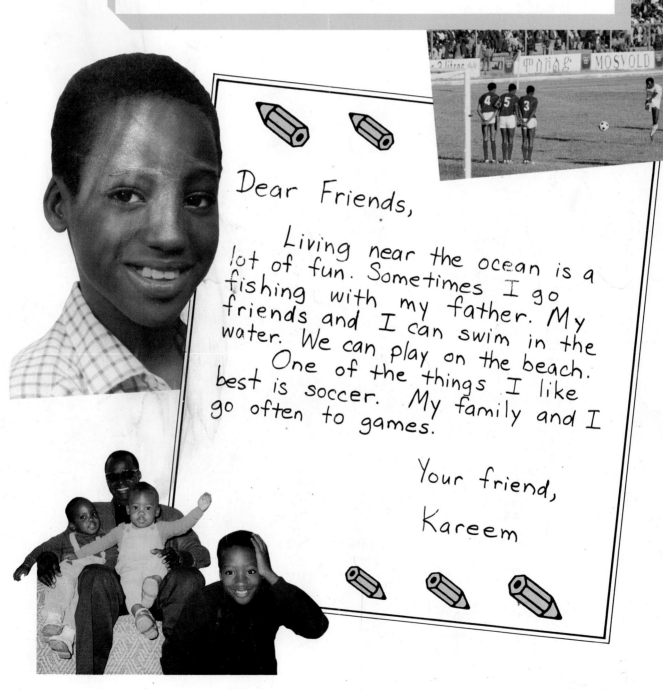

Dear Friends,

Living near the ocean is a lot of fun. Sometimes I go fishing with my father. My friends and I can swim in the water. We can play on the beach.

One of the things I like best is soccer. My family and I go often to games.

Your friend,

Kareem

Saturday is market day in Monrovia. That is when people buy and sell at an outdoor market. Some people bring food from their farms to sell. Some make baskets. Kareem's mother is a weaver. A weaver makes cloth. Sometimes she sells tie-dyed cloth at the market.

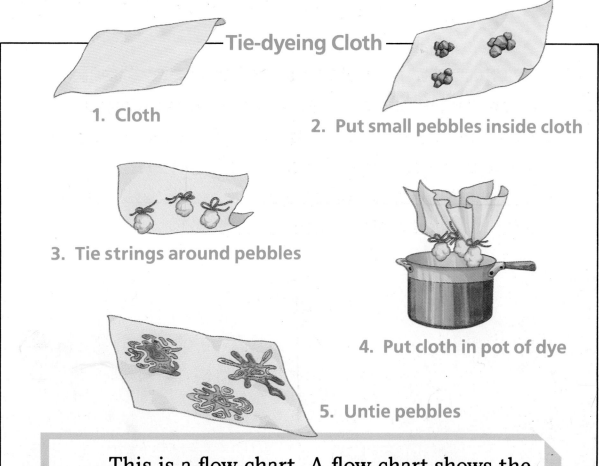

Tie-dyeing Cloth

1. Cloth

2. Put small pebbles inside cloth

3. Tie strings around pebbles

4. Put cloth in pot of dye

5. Untie pebbles

This is a flow chart. A flow chart shows the steps in making something. This flow chart shows how Kareem's mother tie-dyes cloth.

Lesson 3

Review

Read and Think

1. On what continent is Monrovia?

2. What things are sold at an outdoor market?

Skills Check

Look at the picture on page 158. Why, do you think, is Saturday a good market day?

Lesson 4

Where Is Jorge's Community?

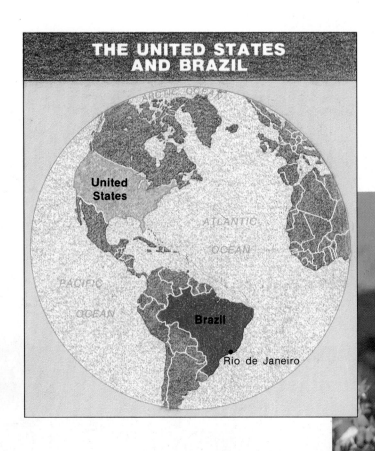

THE UNITED STATES AND BRAZIL

Jorge lives in a farming community near Rio de Janeiro, Brazil. Brazil is the largest country in South America.

Jorge's parents are farmers. They grow bananas, corn, and beans. Jorge likes to help his father in the field. When the crops are ready, they sell them in Rio de Janeiro.

Rio de Janeiro is often called Rio. It is a beautiful city. It has ocean on one side and mountains on the other. Rio has many libraries and museums. People come from all over the world to visit them.

It is always warm in Rio. Jorge and his family can go to the beach year-round.

Review

Read and Think

1. On what continent is the country of Brazil?
2. Why can Jorge visit the beach year-round in Rio?

Skills Check

Write two sentences telling something you have learned about Brazil.

A. Using the New Words

Find the picture that best matches each word.

1. globe _____
2. ocean _____
3. continent _____
4. mountain _____
5. island _____
6. hill _____
7. lake _____
8. river _____

A.

B.

C.

D.

E.

F.

G.

H.

B. Remembering What You Read

1. Where do all people live?

2. How are hills and mountains different?

3. What are the names of two continents?

C. Summarizing the Unit

Number a sheet of paper from **1** to **6**. Find the number 1 in the picture. Find the word that fits number 1. Write the word on your paper.

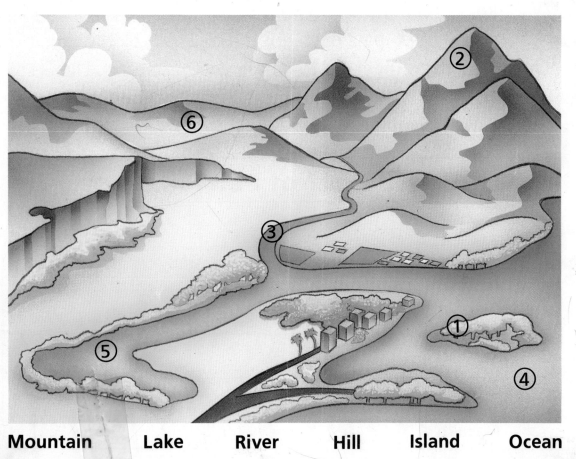

Mountain   Lake   River   Hill   Island   Ocean

SKILLBUILDER

Reading Bar Graphs

A Why Do I Need This Skill?

A bar graph is a special kind of drawing that shows how much or how many. Bar graphs can show information in a clear and easy way.

B Learning the Skill

Masako, Kareem, and Jorge have pen pals. The bar graph shows how many pen pals each child has. Point to the name Masako. Slide your finger up to where the bar stops. The number to the left means that Masako has two pen pals. How many do Kareem and Jorge have?

Number of Pen Pals

5			
4			
3			
2			
1			
	Masako	Kareem	Jorge

166

Practicing the Skill

A second-grade class made a bulletin board about our country. Visitors came to see the bulletin board. Use the bar graph below to answer these questions.

1. How many visitors came on Tuesday?
2. On which day did the most visitors come?
3. What was the greatest number of visitors in one day?

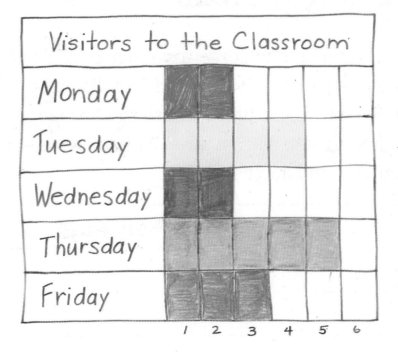

Visitors to the Classroom

 Applying the Skill

Your classmates have a total of 17 pets. There are 8 dogs, 6 cats, and 3 birds. Draw a bar graph, using this information.

167

New Words

President

Congress

flag

pledge

How Is Our Country Governed?

Our country has a special leader. That leader is the **President**. The President is part of our country's government.

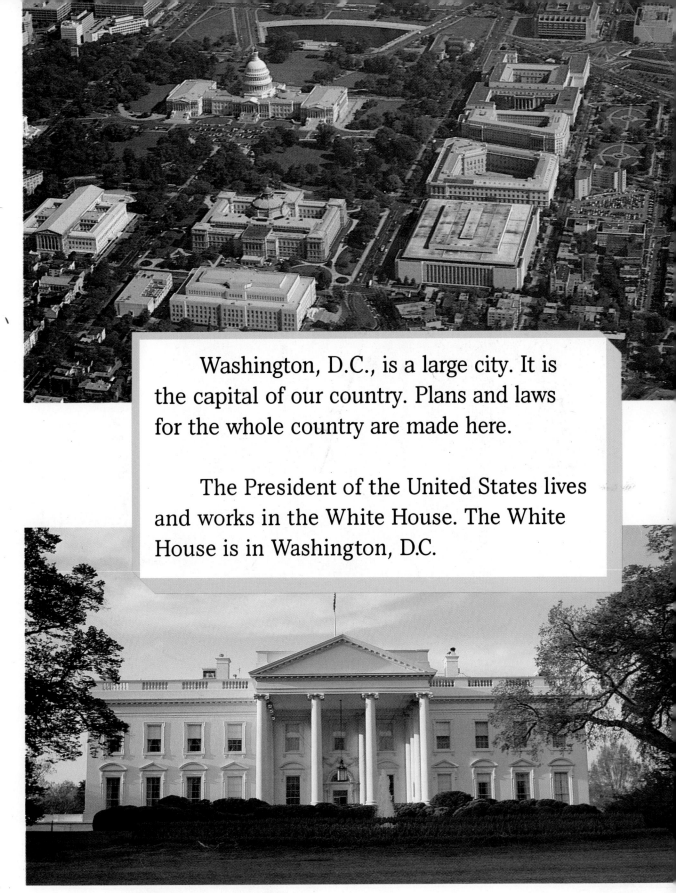

Washington, D.C., is a large city. It is the capital of our country. Plans and laws for the whole country are made here.

The President of the United States lives and works in the White House. The White House is in Washington, D.C.

The President and members of **Congress** make plans and laws for our country. Congress is made up of a group of men and women from each state. The people in each state choose leaders to be members of Congress.

This is the capitol building. It is in Washington, D.C. Members of Congress meet and work in this building.

Review

Read and Think

1. Who is the leader of our country?
2. Who helps our President make plans and laws for the country?

Skills Check

Imagine you are a visitor to the White House. Write a sentence telling about your visit.

Lesson 2

What Are Some Symbols of Our Country?

One of the most important symbols of our country is the American **flag**. We are proud of our flag. We honor it when we say the **Pledge** of Allegiance. This pledge is a promise to be true to our country.

174

When we say the pledge to our flag, we stand and face the flag. We place our right hand over our heart and say the following words.

I pledge allegiance to the flag
of the United States of America
and to the republic for which it stands,
one nation under God, indivisible,
with liberty and justice for all.

The picture shows our first flag. Long ago our country had 13 states. Our first flag had 13 stars and 13 stripes. A star and a stripe stood for each state. Today our flag still has 13 stripes to honor our first 13 states. But now our flag has 50 stars. Each star stands for one of the 50 states in our country.

These are symbols of our country too.
They are the Statue of Liberty, the Great Seal,
and the American bald eagle.

The most important thing about our country is the people. We are all Americans. We all helped to make our country great.

We are proud to be Americans. The United States of America is a great place to live.

Lesson 2 ——————————— Review ————————

Read and Think

1. How many stripes does our flag have?
2. What are some places that fly the flag?

Skills Check

Look at the pictures on page 174. What are the children doing?

What Does Our Country Look Like?

Our country is the United States of America. It is a very special place. No other place is just like our country. The United States has many natural features.

If you took a trip across the
United States, these are some of the
natural features you might see.

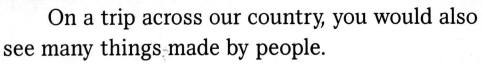

On a trip across our country, you would also see many things made by people.

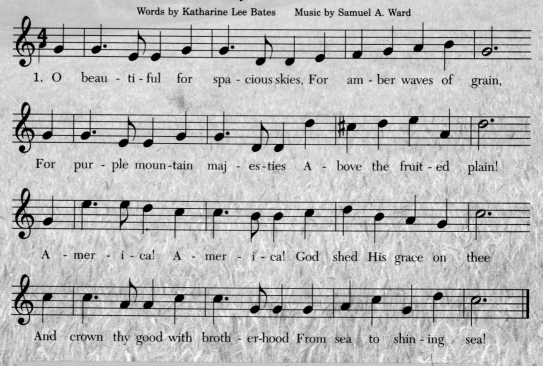

America, the Beautiful

Words by Katharine Lee Bates   Music by Samuel A. Ward

1. O beau-ti-ful for spa-cious skies, For am-ber waves of grain,

For pur-ple moun-tain maj-es-ties A-bove the fruit-ed plain!

A-mer-i-ca! A-mer-i-ca! God shed His grace on thee

And crown thy good with broth-er-hood From sea to shin-ing sea!

The song "America, the Beautiful" tells about the beauty of our country.

Lesson 4

Review

Read and Think

1. What are some natural features in our country?
2. What are some natural features in your state?

Skills Check

Look at the pictures on pages 180 and 181. What natural features can you identify?

Conserving Natural Resources

Adam wanted a drink of water. He turned on the faucet. He let the water run and run. Adam's mother heard the water running.

"Why is the water running for so long?" asked his mother.

"I want it to get cold before I drink it," replied Adam.

His mother said, "Water is an important resource. We must use only what we need. This way we can conserve it."

"What does conserve mean?" asked Adam.

"Conserve means not spoiling or wasting but using wisely," said his mother.

Then Adam's mother gave him water from the refrigerator. She told Adam that it is important to conserve all of our resources.

Water is one of our most important natural resources. Air, land, and trees are also very important. We use many natural resources every day. But we must be careful how we use them.

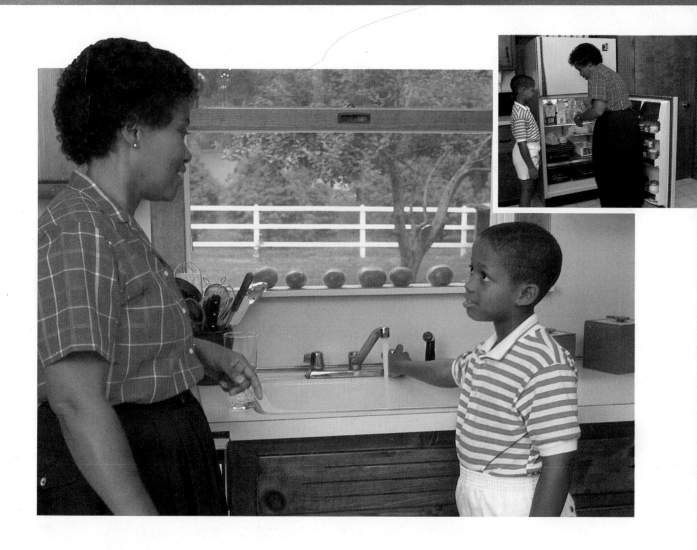

Thinking for Yourself

Everyone needs water. It is a natural resource people cannot live without. It is up to everyone to use water wisely.

1. What are some ways you use water?
2. What are some ways you can save water?
3. Why is it important to care for our resources?

A. Using the New Words

Find the picture that best matches each word.

1. President   _____
2. Congress   _____
3. flag   _____
4. pledge   _____

A.

B.

C.

D.

B. Remembering What You Read

1. Who is the leader of our country?
2. Where does the President live?
3. What are some symbols of our country?

C. Summarizing the Unit

Look at the two flags and answer these questions.
1. Which is our country's first flag?
2. How is the new flag different from the first flag?
3. In what ways are both flags the same?

Draw and color a picture of our flag.

SKILLBUILDER

Identifying the Seasons

A Why Do I Need This Skill?

In some places the weather stays the same all year round. In other places it changes during the year. The changes in the weather make four seasons. Knowing the seasons helps you plan what to wear and plan the things you can do.

B Learning the Skill

A season is a time of year. The four seasons are spring, summer, fall, and winter. In spring the weather gets warmer. Plants begin to grow. Flowers begin to bloom.

Summer follows spring. Summer is the hottest season. Days are longer too.

In fall the days get cooler. Leaves change color and fall to the ground.

Winter is the coldest season. In many places there is ice and snow.

Spring	Summer	Fall	Winter

C Practicing the Skill

Look at the pictures of the four seasons on page 188. Then answer the following questions.

1. During what season is the weather the hottest?
2. During what season do some trees drop their leaves?
3. Which season is the coldest?
4. During what season does the weather start to get warm?

D Applying the Skill

Look at the picture below. Pretend you are visiting this place. Answer the following questions.

1. What kind of clothing would you wear?
2. What are some things you would do for fun?
3. What is the weather like?
4. What season do you think it is?

Unit 8 HOLIDAYS PEOPLE CELEBRATE

New Words

Pilgrims

feast

celebrate

monument

190

Why Do We Celebrate Thanksgiving?

The Granger Collection

Thanksgiving is a time for remembering our country's past. Long ago the **Pilgrims** came to live in our country. The Pilgrims were a group of settlers from England.

The first winter was very hard for the Pilgrims. American Indians living nearby helped them. The Indians showed the Pilgrims how to grow crops. When the crops were ready, the Pilgrims were thankful. They decided to **celebrate**. They shared a **feast** with the Indians. A feast is a special dinner.

The Pilgrims thanked God for their new home, their food, and their new friends. That was our country's first Thanksgiving.

Thanksgiving is also celebrated in Canada. Jimmy tells about this holiday in his letter.

Dear Friends,

I live in Canada. We celebrate Thanksgiving here too. It is an important day in my country. Thanksgiving was first celebrated by farmers. They wanted to give thanks for the good growing season. Today, Thanksgiving is a holiday all over Canada.

In Canada, Thanksgiving is the second Monday in October. We have a big dinner. Sometimes friends and relatives come. Thanksgiving is my favorite holiday.

Your friend,

Jimmy

194

Today, Americans celebrate Thanksgiving on the fourth Thursday in November. It is a day for giving thanks to God for all the things we have. It is also a day to have fun. These people are enjoying a parade.

Lesson 1 — Review

Read and Think

1. Where did the Pilgrims come from?
2. Why, do you think, is Thanksgiving celebrated in the fall?

Skills Check

Look at the picture on page 193. Explain what you think the Pilgrims and Indians are doing.

Thanksgiving Day

By LYDIA MARIA CHILD

This poem is about a family's trip to visit grandparents on Thanksgiving Day.

Over the river and through the wood,
To grandfather's house we go;
The horse knows the way
To carry the sleigh
Through the white and drifted snow.

Over the river and through the wood—
Oh, how the wind does blow!
It stings the toes
And bites the nose,
As over the ground we go.

Over the river and through the wood
   Trot fast, my dapple-gray!
      Spring over the ground,
      Like a hunting hound!
For this is Thanksgiving Day.

Over the river and through the wood,
   And straight to the barnyard gate.
      We seem to go
      Extremely slow,—
It is so hard to wait!

Over the river and through the wood,
   Now grandmother's cap I spy!
      Hurrah for the fun!
      Is the pudding done?
Hurrah for the pumpkin pie!

What Do You Think?

    Write a paragraph telling about this family's
Thanksgiving Day trip. Tell about the weather and
how the family dressed for the trip.

Why Do We Remember Dr. Martin L. King, Jr.?

Dr. Martin Luther King, Jr., was born on January 15, 1929, in Atlanta, Georgia.

Dr. King spent his life fighting for the rights of other people. Today, Americans remember Dr. King on the third Monday in January.

Dr. King had a dream for our country. He wanted all people to be treated fairly.

Dr. King worked hard to make his dream come true. He became a leader in our country. He spoke to large crowds of people. He led a large group of people to Washington, D.C. They asked our government leaders for fair treatment and equality for all Americans.

Lesson 2 ——— Review ———

Read and Think
1. In what state was Dr. King born?
2. Why was Dr. King a good American citizen?

Skills Check
Find Georgia on the map on pages 84 and 85. What state is below Georgia on the map?

What Makes a Great Leader?

As you learned in Lesson 2, Dr. King was a great leader. He helped America become a better place for all people. But how did Dr. King become such an important person?

As a young boy, Martin wanted to be like his father. Martin watched his father help people in many ways. He listened to his father speak in church and chose to become a pastor himself.

Dr. King felt that some laws were unfair to African Americans and that they should be changed. He decided to do something about the laws. Dr. King asked people to show they were against unfair laws without using violence. He believed in nonviolence, or acting peacefully.

Because of Dr. King many unfair laws in our country were changed. In 1964 he was awarded the Nobel Prize for Peace.

Thinking for Yourself

1. What can you do to help others?
2. What can you do to help your country?
3. Do you put forth your best effort for something you think is right?

What Is Presidents' Day?

George Washington and Abraham Lincoln were two great American Presidents. Both were born in February. Each year we honor them on Presidents' Day.

George Washington was a leader. Long ago he helped Americans win their freedom from England. The American people admired Washington. They made him the first President of our country. President Washington helped to set up a plan for making rules and laws for our country. He helped the United States become a strong nation.

The Granger Collection

The Granger Collection

Abraham Lincoln was our sixteenth President. When he became President, our country was divided. Some states let people own other people. This is known as slavery. The President and many other Americans believed that slavery was wrong. Lincoln worked hard to bring the country together and to end slavery.

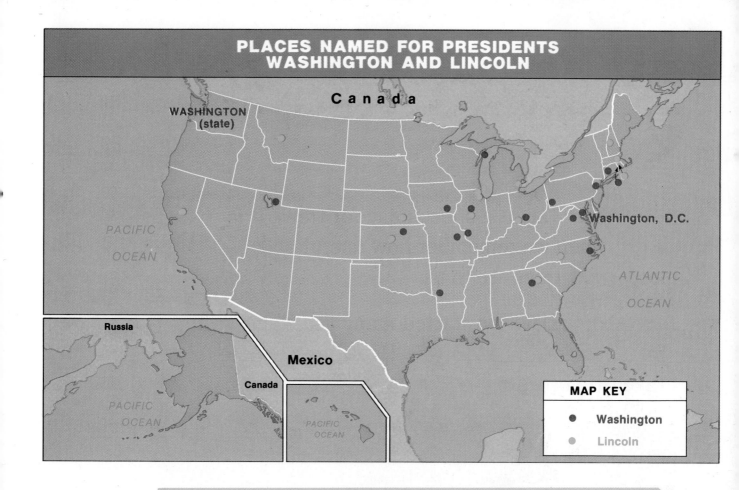

PLACES NAMED FOR PRESIDENTS
WASHINGTON AND LINCOLN

Canada

WASHINGTON
(state)

PACIFIC
OCEAN

Washington, D.C.

ATLANTIC
OCEAN

Russia

Mexico

Canada

PACIFIC
OCEAN

PACIFIC
OCEAN

MAP KEY

●   Washington

●   Lincoln

These are some of the places named
for Lincoln and Washington. There are
buildings and **monuments** named for them too.

Lesson 3

Review

Read and Think

1. Who do we honor on Presidents' Day?
2. In what month is Presidents' Day celebrated?

Skills Check

Look at the map on this page. Which president has
a state named for him?

What Is Arbor Day?

Arbor Day is a special day for trees. It is a day when we remember how useful and important trees are to us.

Arbor Day was started many years ago by a man named Julius Morton. He wanted people to take care of trees.

Mrs. Reed's class is celebrating Arbor Day. The children have drawn trees for their Arbor Day bulletin board.

Mrs. Reed took the children outside. They looked at some live trees.

Trees have many uses. They give us good things to eat, such as these nuts. They give us fruits too. They help make our country beautiful. Many animals like these make their homes in trees.

Some people plant a tree on Arbor Day. Some like to go out and look at different kinds of trees. In many schools the children learn how to care for trees.

Lesson 4
Review

Read and Think
1. Who started Arbor Day?
2. Name an animal that makes its home in a tree.

Skills Check
Look at the picture on page 206. What kind of tree do you think this is?

A. Using the New Words

Find the picture that best matches each word.

1. Pilgrims ____
2. feast ____
3. celebrate ____
4. monument ____

A.

B.

C.

D.

B. Remembering What You Read

1. Where did the Pilgrims come from?
2. What are some things people do on Arbor Day?
3. What is your favorite holiday?

C. Summarizing the Unit

Copy the chart below onto a sheet of paper. Write at least one thing people do on each holiday.

HOLIDAY CHART	
HOLIDAY	**THINGS PEOPLE LIKE TO DO**
Thanksgiving Day	
Dr. Martin Luther King's Birthday	
Presidents' Day	
Arbor Day	

Using Time Lines

 A # Why Do I Need This Skill?

A time line is a special kind of drawing. It shows when things happened. A time line also shows the order in which something happened.

 B # Learning the Skill

You read a time line from left to right. The event on the left happened first. The event on the right happened later.

Look at the time line below. It shows the days of the week. Sunday is the first day of the week. Saturday is the last day. What are the second and third days of the week?

Days-of-the-Week Time Line						
Sunday	Monday	Tuesday	Wednesday	Thursday	Friday	Saturday

Practicing the Skill

This time line shows the 12 months in a year. Read the time line from left to right. Which month is first? Which month is last?

Months-of-the-Year Time Line

January | February | March | April | May | June | July | August | September | October | November | December

Applying the Skill

Copy the time line onto a sheet of paper. Add the following events to the time line. Put an X mark where these events fall.

1. The month you were born
2. The month school opens
3. The month it is now
4. The month Thanksgiving comes in
5. The month school closes

ATLAS

THE UNITED STATES OF AMERICA

MAP KEY

- ⊛ National capital
- ⊛ State capitals
- • Other cities

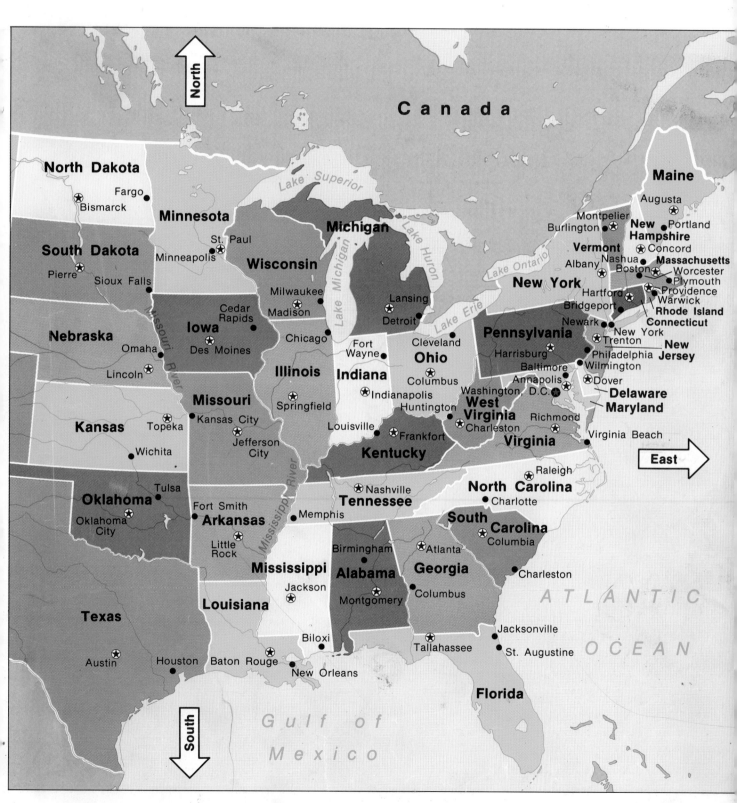

North

Canada

North Dakota
⊛ Fargo
Bismarck ●

Minnesota
St. Paul ⊛
Minneapolis ●

South Dakota
Pierre ⊛
● Sioux Falls

Michigan
Lake Superior

Maine
Augusta ⊛
Montpelier ●⊛ Portland ●
Burlington ● **New Hampshire**
Vermont ⊛ Concord
Albany Nashua ⊛ **Massachusetts**
⊛ Boston ⊛⊛ Worcester
New York Hartford ● Plymouth
● Providence ⊛
Bridgeport ● Warwick ●
Newark ● **Rhode Island**
⊛ **Connecticut**
New York ●
Trenton ⊛ **New**
Philadelphia ●⊛ **Jersey**
⊛ Wilmington
Annapolis ● ⊛ Dover
⊛ **Delaware**
Washington, D.C.⊛ **Maryland**

Wisconsin
Milwaukee ●
Madison ⊛
Lansing ●
⊛ Detroit ●
Lake Michigan
Lake Huron
Lake Ontario
Lake Erie

Cedar
Rapids ●
Iowa
Des Moines ⊛
Chicago ●
Fort
Wayne ● Cleveland ●
Ohio
Columbus ⊛
Indiana
⊛ Indianapolis
Huntington

Nebraska
Omaha ●
Lincoln ⊛

Missouri River

Illinois
Springfield ⊛

Harrisburg ⊛
Pennsylvania
Baltimore ●

Missouri
Kansas City ●
Jefferson ⊛
City
Louisville ●
⊛ Frankfort
West Virginia
⊛ Charleston

Richmond ⊛

Kansas
Topeka ⊛
Wichita ●

Kentucky

Virginia
● Virginia Beach

East

Mississippi River

⊛ Nashville
Tennessee
Memphis ●
● Raleigh
North Carolina
● Charlotte

Oklahoma
Tulsa ●
Oklahoma ⊛
City
Fort Smith
⊛ **Arkansas**
Little
Rock ⊛

South Carolina
Columbia ⊛
● Charleston

Birmingham ●
Alabama
⊛ Atlanta
Georgia

Mississippi
Jackson ⊛
Montgomery ⊛
Columbus ●

Texas
Austin ⊛
Houston ● Baton Rouge ●
Louisiana
● Biloxi
New Orleans ●

Jacksonville ●
● St. Augustine
Tallahassee ⊛

Florida

ATLANTIC

OCEAN

South

Gulf of
Mexico

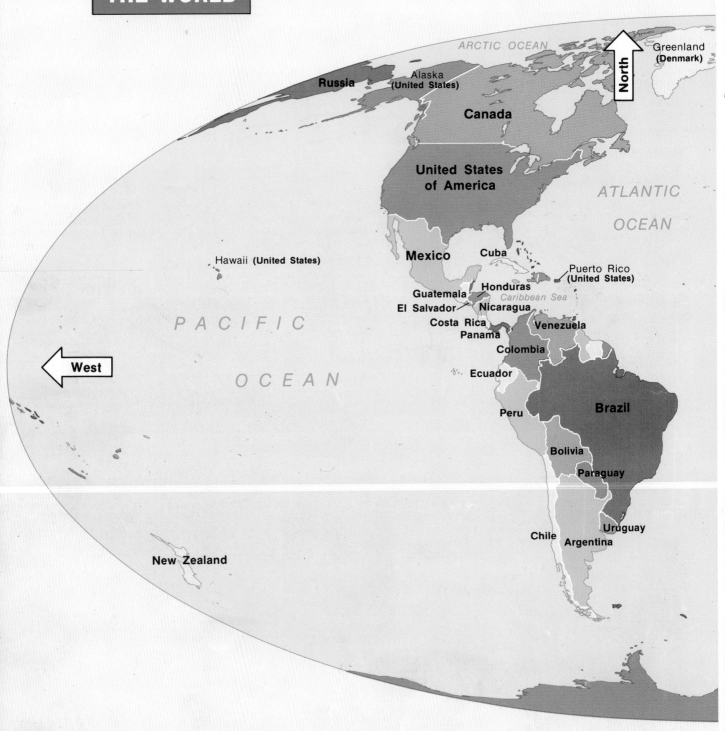

ARCTIC OCEAN

North

Greenland
(Denmark)

Russia

Alaska
(United States)

Canada

United States
of America

ATLANTIC

OCEAN

Hawaii (United States)

Mexico

Cuba

Puerto Rico
(United States)

Honduras

Caribbean Sea

Guatemala

Nicaragua

El Salvador

Venezuela

Costa Rica

Panama

Colombia

PACIFIC

Ecuador

West

Brazil

OCEAN

Peru

Bolivia

Paraguay

Uruguay

Chile   Argentina

New Zealand

ARCTIC OCEAN

Iceland

Norway

Finland

Sweden

Denmark

United Kingdom

Ireland

Poland

Czechoslovakia

France

Romania

Yugoslavia

Bulgaria

Portugal

Spain

Italy

Greece

Turkey

Mediterranean Sea

Tunisia

Syria

Afghanistan

Morocco

Iraq

Jordan

Iran

Pakistan

Algeria

Libya

Egypt

Qatar

Saudi Arabia

Mauritania

Mali

Niger

Chad

Sudan

Senegal

Gambia

Guinea

Sierra Leone

Liberia

Nigeria

Ethiopia

Ivory Coast

Ghana

Cameroon

Somalia

Gabon

Zaire

Kenya

Tanzania

Angola

Zambia

Malawi

Madagascar

South Africa

Russia

China

North Korea

South Korea

Japan

Taiwan

PACIFIC OCEAN

Bangladesh

India

Myanmar

Laos

Thailand

Vietnam

Sri Lanka

Philippines

Malaysia

East

INDIAN OCEAN

Indonesia

ATLANTIC OCEAN

Australia

Sydney

South

DICTIONARY OF PLACES

You can find each place on a map in your book. The pages tell you where the maps are.

Africa

One of the earth's seven continents.
Pages 148–149

Atlanta

A city in the state of Georgia. Pages 84–85

Antarctica

One of the earth's seven continents.
Pages 148–149

Atlantic Ocean

The largest body of salt water along the eastern coast of the United States.
Pages 148–149

Arctic Ocean

The largest body of salt water near the North Pole.
Pages 148–149

Australia

The earth's smallest continent.
Pages 148–149

Asia

The earth's largest continent.
Pages 148–149

Baltimore

The largest city in the state of Maryland.
Pages 214–215

Brazil

A country in South America. Page 160

Florida

A state in the southern part of the United States. Pages 84–85

Canada

The country that is directly north of the United States. Page 150

Georgia

A state in the southern part of the United States. Pages 84–85

Colorado

A state in the western part of the United States. Pages 84–85

Indian Ocean

A body of salt water between Africa and Asia. Pages 148–149

England

Part of the United Kingdom. The Pilgrims came from England. Pages 216-217

Japan

An island country that is part of the continent of Asia. Page 152

Europe

The earth's second smallest continent. Pages 148–149

Liberia

A country on the continent of Africa. Page 156

DICTIONARY OF PLACES

Maryland

A state that borders on the Atlantic Ocean. Pages 84–85

North America

The earth's third largest continent. Page 150

Massachusetts

A state that borders on the Atlantic Ocean. Pages 84–85

Oklahoma

A state that borders on six other states. Pages 84–85

Mexico

A country that is directly south of the United States. Page 150

Oregon

A state that borders on the Pacific Ocean. Page 83

Monrovia

The capital city of Liberia. Page 156

Pacific Ocean

The earth's largest body of salt water. It is off the west coast of the United States. Pages 148–149

New Jersey

A state that borders on the Atlantic Ocean. Pages 84–85

Plymouth

The second oldest English settlement in America. Plymouth is in Massachusetts. Pages 214–215

Rio de Janeiro

A city in Brazil.
Page 160

St. Augustine

A city in Florida. It is the oldest city in the United States.
Pages 214–215

South America

The earth's fourth largest continent.
Pages 148–149

Sydney

A city on the continent of Australia.
Pages 216–217

Tokyo

The capital city of Japan. Page 152

Trenton

The capital city of the state of New Jersey.
Pages 84–85

United States of America

Our country, that stretches from the Atlantic Ocean to the Pacific Ocean.
Pages 84–85

Virginia

A state in the southern part of the United States.
Pages 84–85

Washington, D.C.

The capital city of the United States.
Pages 84–85

PICTURE GLOSSARY

The page numbers tell where each word first appears in the text.

The page numbers tell where each word first appears in the text.

B

basic needs

Things that all people must have to live. p. 94.

budget

A spending plan to help people decide how to use their money. p. 102.

buffalo

A large animal that lived in great numbers on the plains of the United States. p. 124.

C

capitol building

A building where leaders of a country or state meet and work. p. 87.

celebrate

Do special things for an event or holiday. p. 193.

city

A large community. p. 47.

community

A place where people live, work, and play. p. 32.

Congress

The men and women chosen to help make laws for all the people in our country. p. 172.

continent

One of the seven large bodies of land on the earth. p. 148.

country

A large area of land and the people who live there. p. 84.

flag

A symbol of a country. p. 174.

D

direction

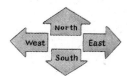

The way in which a person or thing faces, points, or moves. p. 43.

G

globe

A model of the earth. p. 144.

dugout canoe

A boat made by hollowing out a large log. p. 123.

governor

A person who is elected by the people of a state to be their leader. p. 86.

F

factory

A place where products are made. p. 108.

graph

A drawing that shows how much or how many. Pie graphs and bar graphs are kinds of graphs. p. 102.

feast

A meal prepared for a special occasion. p. 193.

PICTURE GLOSSARY

group  A number of people together. p. 22.

H

hill  A place where the land is high. p. 147.

I

income  The money people earn for the work they do. p. 98.

island  A body of land that has water all around it. p. 147.

L

lake  A body of water with land all around it. p. 146.

law  A rule that people must obey. p. 72.

leader  A person who leads a group of people. p. 76.

M

map  A drawing of the earth or part of the earth. p. 36.

map key A part of a map that explains the symbols used on a map. p. 37.

Map Key

- 🏠 House
- 〰️ Lake
- ✈️ Airport
- 🚌 School

mayor
The most important leader in a community. p. 77.

monument
A building or statue built to honor a person or event. p. 205.

mountain
Very high land that rises above the land around it. p. 147.

natural resources
Things in nature that people use. p. 120.

neighborhood
A small part of a community. p. 33.

O

ocean
A very large body of salt water. There are four oceans on earth. p. 146.

P

Pilgrims
A group of people who came to America and settled in Massachusetts. p. 192.

pioneer
A person who leads the way to a new land. p. 132.

pledge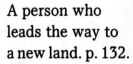
A promise. p. 174.

PICTURE GLOSSARY

President

The most important leader of the United States. p. 170.

product

Something that is made or grown and sold. Food and clothes are products. p. 99.

R

river

A long body of water that flows through the land. p. 146.

rule

What you may or may not do. p. 68.

S

senses

The special parts of the body that let us see, hear, feel, taste, and smell. p. 8.

service

Something someone does for others. p. 100.

settlement

A small community. p. 131.

settler

A person who came from another country to live in America. p. 130.

226

PICTURE GLOSSARY

share  Giving a part of what is yours to someone else. p. 5.

transportation  The way people or products travel from one place to another. p. 52.

state  One of the 50 parts of the United States. p. 82.

Arkansas

tribe  A large group of people living together who share the same beliefs, such as a tribe of American Indians. p. 120.

suburb  A community near a city. p. 47.

symbol  A drawing or object that stands for something real. p. 37.

V

vote  How someone helps to choose a leader. p. 78.

T

W

taxes  Money people pay to a community or government. p. 106.

wants  Things that people would like to have but do not need to live. p. 97.

INDEX

CREDITS

Ariana Walker